NewLaw New Rules

A conversation about the future of the legal services industry

By George Beaton

Illustrations by Julian Jones

Published by Beaton Capital Pty Ltd

(ACN 141 049 916)

Melbourne, Australia

Smashwords Edition

DEDICATION

To Margaret

TABLE OF CONTENTS

FOREWORD

Never, in the history of the legal blogosphere, have so many innovators, disruptors, gurus, and rebels assembled in one shared space. George Beaton is to be warmly congratulated for hosting and generating such a lively and informed conversation about tomorrow's law firms. In the best spirit of peer production, with echoes too of rapid-fire Socratic exchange, the contributors have co-created an e-book that asks and largely answers the key strategic questions that all law firm leaders must now be invited to address. This is mandatory reading for anyone who is interested in legal businesses of the future.

Professor Richard Susskind OBE

ACKNOWLEDGEMENTS

NewLaw New Rules is the result of supreme team work. My thanks go first to the 35 contributors – without their insights and energy, there would be no NewLaw New Rules. Professor Richard Susskind, rightly famous for his books on the future of lawyers, was kind enough to write the Foreword to NewLaw New Rules.

Our Melbourne-based project team was more than ably led by Dr Imme Kaschner, a recent JD graduate of the Melbourne Law School. In addition to managing the team, Imme expertly shouldered the compilation of the material. She harnessed Eric Chin, Senior Analyst in Beaton Capital and Beaton Research + Consulting, Julian Jones, Senior Designer, Dr Ryan Wallman, Head of Copy at Wellmark, Lynda Dean, Consultant Support Manager, Beaton Research + Consulting and – Imme's biggest challenge – me.

A special word of appreciation is reserved for Eric Chin's thoughtfulness and diligence in contributing to this thread book and ideas for its sequel.

To the Tweet authors, thank you for unwittingly adding colour and pith to the commentary. You ensured the word kept spreading as the thread gathered pace around the world; without yours and others' tweets, NewLaw New Rules would be the poorer.

A note on language. The contributors write and spell in American, Australian, British, Canadian and Spanish forms of English. In the direct quotations used in NewLaw New Rules, the author's language has not been standardised, or is it standardized?

George Beaton

CHAPTER 1.
INTRODUCTION

It began with 'The rise and rise of the NewLaw business model' posted on 7 October 2013 on Bigger. Better. Both?, The Beaton Capital Blog. In that post, I canvassed recent developments in the legal services industry, specifically the rise of providers that do not fit the traditional law firm mould.

The ensuing discussion about current and anticipated developments in the legal services sector attracted responses from law firm leaders, practitioners, consultants and academics. In the blogosphere and on Twitter contributors from Australia, Canada, Hong Kong, Spain, the United Kingdom and the United States engaged in vigorous and insightful exchanges. The intensity and pace of the discussion over the course of two months attested to the timeliness of the questions that were being raised. And there was certainly a common theme: Major changes are afoot in how clients are buying legal services and how providers are innovating and responding – and in some cases appear not to be responding.

Notwithstanding disagreement about their exact nature and consequences, the commentators all recognised major and accelerating changes in the demand and supply sides of the legal services industry. As the discussion unfolded amongst participants with many different perspectives and each offering well-considered opinions, it became obvious that the content of the discussion deserved to be made widely available and in a more accessible format. This would allow the themes to emerge more clearly and the issues to be brought into sharper focus.

This book is an anthology; it collates, curates and comments on the authors' views. The book aims to preserve the essential content and tone of the independent contributions and spirited exchanges, at the same time allowing for easy reference to parts of the debate relating to specific topics. I have included the numbers of the comments and replies in the original blog thread which remains available for reference. These numbers are shown in parentheses, eg (#27.2).

NewLaw New Rules is a 'thread' book. It has been crowd-sourced and is based on an initial post that sparked a torrent of comments and replies. These have been supplemented and linked with other posts and my narrative. As such it may represent a new genre in publishing. Consistent with the contemporary ethos of the internet, publication of NewLaw New Rules relies on trust; the hallmark of good web-based communication and commerce. Starting on 12 November 2013 NewLaw New Rules was conceived, written, illustrated and published in five weeks.

EVOLUTION

The curse about living in interesting times is a fitting reference to the many and novel changes occurring in the legal services industry. This first chapter considers the role of disruption and innovation diffusion. Broadly, the business model adopted by almost all law firms (styled 'BigLaw') since the early 20th century is being challenged. Clients are changing their buying behaviour and newcomers (styled 'NewLaw') with different business models, external investors, fixed fees and other distinctive features are engaged in the contest. These trends are set out in Chapter 2.

The development of these NewLaw business model firms has occurred over the last 20 years or more, starting with firms like CPA Global and Epoq and ranging through providers such as Axiom Law, founded in 2000, and Riverview Law, established in 2012.

Throughout this book, I use the terms 'BigLaw' and 'NewLaw' to refer to business models. BigLaw and NewLaw do not refer to the size of firms or when they were founded, respectively. BigLaw and NewLaw are distinct and fundamentally different business models.

The phrase Big Law (two words) has been in use – mainly in the USA – for some time. It describes large law firms and by inference their business model. The late Larry Ribstein of the University of Illinois College of Law wrote 'The Death of Big Law' in 2010. This major paper captured the prevailing understanding of the concerns about Big Law. I adopted the words Big Law and removed the space between them to create 'BigLaw' as a mnemonic for the business model underpinning the operations of traditional law firms. No previous authors have explicitly analysed the business model in the way I have. As a business model, BigLaw applies to law firms of all sizes, except solo and micro firms. Chapters 3 and 4 contain more detail on BigLaw.

Weeks after I started using BigLaw to describe the traditional law firm business model, **Eric Chin** coined 'NewLaw' in his provocative post '2018: The year Axiom becomes the world's largest legal services firm'. Eric's NewLaw neologism is a collective noun describing legal services providers with new business models. Chapters 5 and 6 contain more detail on NewLaw.

It was my contrast between BigLaw, the traditional law firm business model, and the NewLaw model that sparked the NewLaw New Rules debate. Chapter 7 highlights some of the important issues facing firms in both categories as we look to the future. George Beaton ('The rise and rise of the NewLaw business model')

The BigLaw business model that includes charging by the billable hour, partner ownership and attraction and training of top legal talent for the partnership track is under challenge from NewLaw firms using distinctly different business models.

The rise and rise of the NewLaw business model

BigLaw is not about large law firms. Nor is NewLaw about new law firms. The issues are much deeper than the size or age of what are colloquially known as law firms. When The Lawyer in London recently published a range of prognostications about the shape and fate of large law firms in 2013 (The Lawyer 'A window into the future'), how many partners in large law firms would have stopped and said to themselves "This is about my future; do I need to do something?" And for those who read the material carefully it couldn't have been very comfortable.

Worrying as the stories in The Lawyer are, I think they miss the real point. The reality of 2018 and beyond will turn out to be a great deal worse and much more varied than The Lawyer and its well-known contributors suggest. And my prognostications apply to all law firms, not just big ones.

Let's start by recapitulating **Eric Chin**'s provocative post 2018: The year Axiom becomes the world's largest legal services firm, set out in detail in Topic 5. OK, Eric shouldn't have inferred that Axiom is a 'law firm'. Axiom doesn't want to be known as a law firm in the traditional mould This makes sense because almost every element of Axiom's, AdventBalance's and others' NewLaw business models are quite different to the business model of BigLaw.

What **Eric** argues is that it is conceivable that Axiom will be larger than DLA Piper or Baker & McKenzie within five years. Axiom is not interested in growth per se.

As a NewLaw business model, clients are rewarding Axiom with their custom. The result is stellar growth, akin to Apple, with year-on-year growth of 30+%.

Recap of the BigLaw business model

The BigLaw business model is built on six elements:

1)   Attraction and training of top legal talent
2)   Leveraging of these full-time lawyers to do the bulk of the work serving clients
3)   Creation of a tournament to motivate the lawyers to strive to become equity partners

(the idea of a tournament is akin to Roman gladiator contests and the subject of Marc Galanter and Thomas Palay's seminal book Tournament of Lawyers)

4)   Tight restrictions on the number of equity owners

5)   Structuring as a partnership and

6)   High hourly rates (which is or at least until very recently has been possible because of the mystique associated with legal advice).

These elements work together to create the economics and culture of the BigLaw business model. No one is more important than another. The only element Axiom and other NewLaw players have in common is part of #1, the attraction of top talent.

In all other respects the NewLaw business model is different. The investors are seeking returns on capital and are separate from the producing staff, so leverage and the tournament are not present.

Certainly some, even many of the staff, have a financial interest in the success of their business, but as an asset, not to maximise equity partners' profits each year. The balance sheets of NewLaw business models are as important as the income statements.

And – most importantly – fees are fixed in NewLaw. The provider, not the client, absorbs the risks of under-estimation and poor matter management.

The NewLaw business model

The NewLaw business model for professional services is now the subject of intense interest. I will only describe a few examples of relevant pieces. The Schumpeter column of The Economist on September 21, 2013 (The Economist 'McKinsey looks set to stay' article) addressed 'The future of the Firm' with the upper case 'F' reserved for McKinsey. In the piece, Schumpeter discussed the challenges facing McKinsey, including a reduced willingness of clients to pay for a few services, including less crucial ones, sold as a single high-priced package by consultancy firms.

Schumpeter also cited an October 2013 Harvard Business Review article, 'Consulting on the cusp of disruption' (Harvard Business Review 'Consulting on the cusp of disruption' article preview) by Clayton Christensen and others as applying to the consulting industry. This article states that firms are quite willing and able to assess the results they receive for their money, despite companies like McKinsey working hard on maintaining their 'opacity' and 'magic'. These forces are similarly at work in regard to law firms. For Australian start-ups challenging parts of McKinsey's business, have a look at Vumero and Expert 360, both following in the e-steps of the Gerson Lehrman Group, a premium virtual platform for connecting clients to experts and their insights.

As I wrote previously, firms like McKinsey are "self-generators of IP and have alliances with leading academic institutions; they don't need scale". But crowd-based providers meet many of the same needs at lower price points. And there's excess capacity. These are the antecedents of disruption.

Like butterflies in the Amazon, virtual and crowd-based professional services firms are starting to disrupt. They are leading the rise and rise of new types of firms and NewLaw, business model.

The different types of the NewLaw business model are discussed in more detail in Chapter 5. In his seminal book The Innovator's Dilemma, Clayton Christensen explored the concept of the dichotomy between sustaining and disruptive innovation. To recap, a disruptive innovation creates a new market and value network, while sustaining and efficiency innovations improve, but do not fundamentally change, existing markets and value networks. Much of the conversation in the thread focused on whether the changes in the legal services market are of an efficiency, sustaining or disruptive nature, and the consequences for the BigLaw business model.

DISRUPTION

One the one hand, the arrival of firms employing different business models seems so far to have had only a small impact on the market for legal services. One the other hand, close analysis of industry dynamics suggests a secular, or structural (i.e. long-term and irreversible), trend that is gathering momentum and will eventually disrupt the market. The factual basis and reasoning behind the potential of the new business models to disrupt traditional firms delivering legal services was the subject of more than one contributor.

In his insightful post (comment #47 in the original thread) **Paul Lippe**, CEO of LegalOnRamp, raised a number of questions that frame an assessment of the disruptive potential of NewLaw firms. He pointed out that an understanding of the current situation necessarily depends on the starting point of the analysis. One version is a view of traditional law firms as being best positioned to address complex legal matters, and since complexity will only increase, their domination of the market will continue. The alternative view is that law is not unique, but rather analogous to other information-dense fields such as music or photography and will therefore be subject to similar processes of digitisation, commoditisation and disruption.

Lippe refuted a simple notion of winners and losers determined by business models. Instead, he pointed to the need to analyse developments in the environment in which law firms exist, such as the nature of matters and client behaviour. This informs decisions about what aspects of business structures should sensibly be adapted. Or put simply, the relevant question for **Lippe** is 'given where you are, what is the sensible next step?'.

Such a view of a mosaic-like disruption, and the need to carefully plan and assess any potential business changes, might be a comforting default option, but it might also result in a lost opportunity to address changes sufficiently quickly and before they reach a tipping point. And the disruption might happen in a faster, more profound way than anticipated by many. **Noah Waisberg** (#27.2) suggested disruptive innovation can hurt even well-managed, responsive firms with considerable investment in research and development, even though **Waisberg** ultimately did not conclude how likely or deep disruption in the legal industry might be. Noah Waisberg (#27.2)

The disc drive / mainframe / workstation / minicomputer makers etc. didn't fail because of poor management. Christensen argues that disruptive innovations can hurt successful, well managed companies that are responsive to their customers and have excellent research and development. (Assuming many law firms fit this.) It is very hard for incumbents to adjust their cost base. That said, I can't tell yet whether Christensen-style disruption will happen with BigLaw, though it could.

Another relevant point was that some types of law firm are more likely to be adversely affected than others. **Mitch Kowalski** saw mid-size firms at most risk in the current conditions. Mitch Kowalski (#24)

The changes happening in the legal services industry are structural, not cyclical.

As we know, better processes and better technology never go away – they are structural in nature, not cyclical. Kodak thought that the market would always want print photography. Instagram showed that the smartest guys in the room at Kodak missed the mark.

When DiligenceEngine's software replaces hordes of associates that traditionally do due diligence, that is structural change.

When MSU perfects qualitative legal prediction and litigators rely on algorithmic prediction based on research that no human can accomplish – that is structural change. It also structurally changes what litigators will actually do – because they'll be going to court even less than they do now.

There will always be room for a very thin band of global firms that have a niche in a high level, narrow band of work – but remember that even the most complex niches become routine after a few years.

The disruption will be most dramatic with the thick middle section (and it is a very thick middle section) of BigLaw that really has no way to differentiate itself. These firms don't do complex work, and they are not niche boutiques – they are stuck in the middle without a plan.

Mitch also gave a <u>video interview</u> about these topics.

Ken Jagger (#23) agreed that mid-size firms might be most at risk in the current legal market, particularly since they provide work on less complex matters that are a prime target for NewLaw firms at this time. Ken Jagger (#23)

Traditional law firms need to restructure their business models to meet client demands.

The comments that resonate with me relate to the ability of very large BigLaw firms to survive and thrive. I don't think there is any doubt about that it may take a while to get to a Big 10 and even longer to get to an Accounting style Big 4 but it seems inevitable.

I believe that it is the AmLaw200 that will not be able to sustain their current structures and are most at risk from the innovators. NewLaw won't be satisfied with low margin/commodity work when there are better ways to undertake complex high margin work as well. What will be fascinating to watch is which of the current players end up in that elite very BigLaw category and how long it takes. Will there be a tipping point where the innovators bust the dam wall open or will it continue to be incremental as it has been to date?

So, while the exact pace of current and impending changes in the legal market is not clear, it seems that firms that are less suited to handling highly complex matters might be most at risk from NewLaw competition at this point.

INNOVATION DIFFUSION

Change is here, and it is here to stay. Yet the mere existence of innovative legal service providers will not automatically result in their use by clients. Traditional law firms have long provided valuable services clients who tend to be risk-averse. **Paul Lippe** (#47) points to the example of email as an available technology that commercial lawyers were very slow to adopt, but which later became pervasive in the industry. I discussed the importance of innovation uptake, early adopters and the importance of critical mass. George Beaton (#20)

Innovation diffusion happens in networks once a critical mass is reached.

Much of the debate in this thread hinges on the extent to which the NewLaw phenomenon is in fact a disruption of the BigLaw-based industry. (Remember that at all times we are discussing business models, not the size of firms).

Unsurprisingly, when we seek to find why disruption is or might be happening, we tend to look for individual pioneers – Henry Ford and Steve Jobs for example. In other words, we may think of Mark Harris, founder of Axiom Law, as a disruptor. But disruption in the sense we are discussing has little to do with brilliant (and perhaps lucky?) individuals. It is primarily a function of networks. If we are to understand disruption, we need to grasp how networks form and operate.

'Epidemic' change occurs when work-a-day clients act in unison, hence the use of my chaos theory "butterfly in the Amazon" reference in the post set out above that sparked this debate.

Solomon Asch's 1950 pioneering research and the 1960's work of Everett Rogers showed human beings have a tendency to follow the herd in particular ways. Readers will recognise the idea of the innovation diffusion curve in which Innovators are followed by Early Adopters who is turn are followed by the Early Majority, etc. Each of these descriptors refers to progressively larger groups of individual buyers and users of the product in question being influenced by those who went before them in trialing the product.

Influence in this sense (i.e. causing an innovation–NewLaw ideas–to diffuse) is a function of an idea taking hold among those who are most receptive to it and, as they increase in numbers, more follow and join in the use of the product. In other words, the innovation tends to build on itself. This is the network effect in action.

Innovators and Early Adopters do not, as individual buyers and users of NewLaw in our case, possess any special qualities. They just need to be interested in learning if their organisations can receive better value from NewLaw than they currently do from BigLaw and be prepared to try it. To the extent they do, they influence others; and the momentum builds. The innovation diffuses.

What determines whether NewLaw in its many manifestations catches on is less who the Innovators and Early Adopters are, and more who those to whom they are connected are. These individuals have higher levels of resistance to the innovation; they are more risk-averse. In other words, Innovators and Early Adopters take the risk and once the superior value of the 'product' is proven, it enters the Early Majority phase. And the chances are it will then go viral in modern parlance. If it doesn't get traction at this point, it's game over and the innovation dies away.

So where is NewLaw in the innovation diffusion curve? My assessment, based on analysis of various indicia, is that NewLaw is still in the first part of the early adopter phase of the innovation diffusion curve. Indicia include but are not limited to the types of clients who are trying – and reusing – NewLaw's services, the growth of NewLaw firms (consider that Axiom Law may be the largest legal services provider in the world by 2018) and the types of lawyers who work in NewLaw enterprises.

Recently it was pointed out in the 3 Geeks and a Law Blog (Three Geeks and a Law Blog 'Not so fast' post) that the railroad revolution in the USA took 50 years to fully disrupt. Author Toby Brown went on to infer that BigLaw may have plenty of time to adjust. I disagree. What is different with NewLaw, and our era is digital technology which has made us all much more connected and drastically shortened product life cycles. What took decades previously now takes years, what took years takes months, and so on.

Conceivably, any firm has the capacity to reinvent itself. If such a firm permanently and sustainably changes elements of the BigLaw business model, then by definition this firm is no longer part of BigLaw. In other words, it will have left the BigLaw strategic group. Is, say, Marque Lawyers of Sydney still a member of the BigLaw strategic group? Marque, as followers of the charismatic Michael Bradley well know, is a first-generation fixed-fee corporate and commercial boutique. My answer is 'yes' – Marque is still BigLaw but has gained itself an advantage over many other BigLaw firms, and bought itself time, by its adoption of fixed fees from its start as a breakaway. Marque may progress further towards NewLaw by changing more elements of its business model in the future.

The literature shows how difficult, if not impossible, it is for a going concern to move out of one strategic group into another. It may be that reinvented BigLaw firms create a new strategic group. Some are certainly trying to escape the trap of BigLaw culture and structure and where they will land is as yet unclear. **Nick Seddon** (#29), while disagreeing with the classification of firms into distinct BigLaw and NewLaw groups, points to the importance of ownership structures in the evolution of law firms, but also suggests that even rapid changes in the legal industry still necessitate fairly long timeframes. Nick Seddon (#29)

The interesting question is what ownership/management structures successful firms will adopt.

In my experience the polarisation between BigLaw and NewLaw firms doesn't really exist. At the opposite ends of the spectrum you might find firms which fit the monikers BigLaw and NewLaw, but what lies in between constitutes a significant part of the legal sector, and it comes in every shade of grey. DLA Piper is presumably BigLaw but was a founder of Riverview Law. NewLaw? Plenty of traditional law firms are moving away from the billable hour and towards the fixed fee without setting up so called NewLaw vehicles.

Yes, we are seeing evolution in the legal sector at a surprising speed but, having just watched David Attenborough's Galapagos, I now understand that evolution at surprising speed still takes years (in the case of the Galapagos, millions).

What I am interested in seeing in the near future within the legal sector is what ownership/management structures providers of legal services adopt. Look at the two different models adopted by the accountants on the one hand and the chartered surveyors on the other, the former still largely using the partnership and the latter incorporated. Both were what you might call BigLaw type partnerships a couple of decades ago. In some ways an equity structure based on shares rather than partnership makes equity more difficult to attain rather than easier.

While there has hardly been a rush by traditional law firms to adopt new structures in Australia (and the same seems to be true to date in the UK and the US), traditional law firms have been seen to show herd mentality. Who predicted the rush of the global players into Australia? So maybe the floodgates have yet to open. We live in interesting times.

So in summary, changing demands in the market for legal services are causing pressure on law firms that operate on the traditional business model. And firms with different business models – that may be more suited to the changing conditions – have sprung up. How much these new business model firms will be able to disrupt the incumbents, and change the landscape of legal services delivery, will depend on the rate and quantity of uptake of their services by clients. It will also depend on the ability of traditional firms to leverage their very considerable strengths while adopting those aspects of NewLaw business models that enable them to continue to serve clients and compete with the newcomers.

USEFUL SOURCES

Beaton, George, 'Firms need reinvention in tough times' on *BRW. Blog* (30 May 2013) http://www.brw.com.au/p/professions/firms_need _reinvention_in_tough_ K3iF3vrenkp2eS1405MdKl

Beaton, George, 'For most law firms, the pyramid has to change' on Beaton Capital, Bigger. Better. Both? (16 February 2013) http://www.beatoncapital.com/2013/02/for-most-law-firms-the-pyramidhas-to-change/

Beaton, George, Interview with Mitch Kowalski (Melbourne, 13 November 2013)< http://www.youtube.com/watch?v=vfPs0dhXf1Q>

Beaton, George, 'Is anything really changing in BigLaw?' on Beaton Capital, Bigger. Better. Both? (19 January 2013) http://www.beatoncapital.com/2013/01/is-anything-really-changing-inbiglaw/

Beaton, George, 'The rise and rise of the NewLaw business model' on Beaton Capital, Bigger. Better. Both? (7 October 2013) http://www.beatoncapital.com/2013/10/rise-rise-newfirm-businessmodel/

Chin, Eric, <u>2018: The year Axiom becomes the world's largest legal services firm</u> on Beaton Capital, Bigger. Better. Both? (1 September 2013) <u>http://www.beatoncapital.com/2013/09/2018-year-axiom-becomesworlds-largest-legal-services-firm/</u>

Christensen, Clayton M, The Innovator's Dilemma (Harvard Business School Press, 1997) Galanter, Mark and Palay, Thomas, Tournament of Lawyers – The Transformation of the Big Law Firm (University of Chicago Press, 1991)

Ribstein, Larry E, '<u>The Death of Big Law</u>' (2010) Wisconsin Law Review 749 <u>http://wisconsinlawreview.org/wp-content/files/1-Ribstein.pdf</u>

Riddell, Warren, 'Big Law at Sea. Red Ocean or Blue Ocean?' on Beaton Capital, Bigger. Better. Both? (1 October 2013) <u>http://www.beatoncapital.com/2013/10/red-ocean-blue-ocean-biglawsea/</u>

CHAPTER 2.
THE LEGAL SERVICES INDUSTRY

Strategic change takes place over long periods of time within an industry structure shaped by many forces. Structural analysis requires consideration of input costs, the basis of incumbent rivalry, client buying behaviour and the threats posed by both new entrants and substitutes. **Andrew Grech** and **Peter Carayiannis** pointed to the complexity of the structure of the legal services industry. **Ron Friedmann** made the argument that what is needed beyond increasing efficiency are risk-adjusted decisions about how much investment in legal services is necessary and asked do 'bigger savings lie in doing less law?'.

Macroeconomic events and trends also influence how industries evolve. **Warren Riddell**, **James Edsberg**, **Peter Kalis** and I referred to economic cycles. There were differing opinions about the materiality of the economic cycle compared to the secular trend, referred to in Chapter 1, in affecting the performance of BigLaw firms.

Comments related to changing client behaviour, including willingness to pay based on billable hours and price-down pressure, were made by **Warren Riddell**, **Peter Carayiannis**, **Mitch Kowalski**, **Patrick Lamb** and **Trish Hyde**. The pressure on in-house counsel to justify their value is increasing the price sensitivity of outside counsel services.

Consumer and small business users of legal services were largely overlooked in the thread. Much of the discussion centered on services provided to larger business. There was, however, some evidence presented on the needs of small to medium businesses and private individuals for better legal services in comment #44.1.

On the supply side, there was discussion on the use of technological tools and processes to enable better, faster and cheaper service delivery. These developments are opening up new types of career opportunities for lawyers, as **Greg Carter** pointed out. **Dan Lear** also provided insight into what these opportunities may look like. And while alternative careers might still seem somewhat risky at the present, **Nicole Bradick** argued that, given time, NewLaw firms which currently rely on BigLaw as their source of lawyers will develop their own talent and reputations as employers in their own ways.

Any type of law firm can, at least theoretically, adopt new technologies, but the presence of so-called legacy systems and risk-aversion in BigLaw firms may limit the degree to which those firms are willing and able to adopt new technologies. The question raised by **Joel Barolsky** – what disruptive technology NewLaw firms would have at their disposal to gain a significant advantage over the incumbents – was considered by **Joshua Kubicki**.

GENERAL TRENDS

Services from BigLaw firms have traditionally been delivered at the highest possible quality – as determined by the lawyers themselves – and mostly remunerated based on the time taken to provide those services. But clients are increasingly questioning both aspects of this behaviour.

Warren Riddell (#12)

'The future isn't what it used to be'. Client power is reshaping the BigLaw business model. BigLaw is in future shock and change is inevitable.

There is one point of view that has been missed so far and that is from the client. I will put it bleakly –

we have seen a secular shift from a seller's market to a buyer's market. We know it is not isolated to law, other professions have suffered this change over the last 25 years, so what that tells me is that it will not reverse. Whether the mystique of law has been blown away, whether it is because clients now know they have a true choice, whether the realisation that it is a homogeneous product in a perfect market and the oceans are turning red – the fact remains that the BigLaw model is now operating in a seller's market.

Joel Barolsky's and others' view that it is a cyclical manifestation must be music to the ears of many partners who are suffering reduced drawings and can't decide how to respond – other than 'just wait, things will be okay'! On the other hand, my discussions with managing partners confirms their view that there has been a structural shift in the market, and that is manifest in the buying behaviours of their clients. Clients now have more choice – that could be a NewLaw alternative, but it could also be from the BigLaw entrants in the Australian market, for example. Just look at the generalist and specialist entrants in the past year or so – they are skimming the high value work.

So how will BigLaw evolve from dominating a seller's market to being subject to a buyer's market? I suggest that gross margins and partners' drawings will fall as investment in differentiation increases, partners' drawings will fall as investment in differentiation increases, and fee rates will be under the pump, whether through the increased use of lower and fixed price arrangements or just by simple price-down pressure relative to the cost of clients' alternatives.

BigLaw will not go away, but as a pervasive species it must be under threat. Some will survive, but most will evolve.

Complex changes are now in play and starting to have adverse effects on BigLaw. Andrew Grech (#44)

Jordan Furlong
@jordan_law21

"Inexorable laws of supply and demand are biting #BigLaw: bit.ly/WG4PNa by @grbeaton_law"

1.45pm Oct 24, 2012

Across the legal services landscape the convergence of evolving client demand (at individual, SME, corporate and government levels), changing client socio-demographics across regions and the emergence of technology which enables services to be delivered with improved value are starting to have a profound impact on the legal profession. The process of change is accelerating and bringing many opportunities to meet clients' needs innovatively, professionally and affordably.

It seems to me that we are all trying to come to terms with what the impact of a convergence between changing client socio-demographics, changing lawyer and workforce aspirations, technology and the availability of alternatives to more traditional (at least for the professions) ownership and business models will be.

My own sense is that the impact will be profound. The signals are now strong that fundamental change is already well entrenched, and this is creating opportunity for some great experimentation. Like all experiments some will succeed and some will fail.

I think like all traditional law firms we are still coming to grips with how we will be able to continue to earn market share in our chosen areas of specialty, but the experimentation has been going strong for the last several years and is starting to deliver some promising and exciting results. It will be interesting to observe how (or whether) the legal profession responds to the opportunities the future will bring.

The following comment similarly draws attention to the need to re-think a legal business model that is not singularly focused on its clients. It also touches on the role of legal talent and the consequences of entrenched legacy information management systems. Peter Carayiannis (#11)

We are witnessing a period of rapid evolution in the business and practice of law. There are evolutionary pressures coming from increasingly sophisticated clients who demand greater efficiency, more transparency, clearer accountability and something other than a 'time and materials' billable hour business model. With time we will see alternative and innovative legal services providers grow and flourish alongside traditional law firms. Those firms that recognise adaptation is the key to survival and everything revolves around providing the best value to the client will benefit.

Our view is that the current situation is not about the end of BigLaw. It is, however, about the ascendency of NewLaw as part of the market for legal services. We have read Professor Christensen's piece on consultants (Editor's note: Consulting on the cusp of disruption') and agree. In our view, a solicitor's practice is the functional equivalent of other types of business consultancies in respect of the business model's key features. We have also read the recent articles on Novus Law – see ABA Journal – 'Who is eating Law Firms' lunch?' – and are well acquainted with their business model.

Clients and a demographic shift with respect to lawyers are driving the changes in the market for legal services. This forum does not allow us to go into a detailed discussion on all of the factors, but any observer of the legal markets throughout the common law nations will have no doubt seen the same trend lines. Corporate clients are no longer satisfied with the status quo, as represented by the billable hour. Not the absolute dollars that are being charged, nor even the business model. We are finally openly talking about the conflict of interest inherent in the billable hour and the incentive to inefficiency that it brings to a traditional law firm.

It is true that a few traditional law firms are adopting innovative billing and developing project management policies. However, let's be perfectly clear, the number of firms that fall into this category represent a minuscule sliver of the total number of firms, at least in the US. Traditional law firms remain tied to a billable hour (read: time and materials) framework. Corporate clients are demanding a new approach, and this means re-engineering not just how we practice law but the financial relationships within the businesses that provide legal services. Law firms are tied to legacy IT systems for which they have paid dearly. Consequently they are not keen to invest in such things as cloud-based solutions. Start-up NewLaw firms are ignoring the legacy systems and moving immediately to the scalable and cost-effective IT solutions that exist in the market today and are passing along the efficiency gains (and cost savings) to their clients.

In terms of demographics, I will leave it to sociologists to explain the mindset of young professionals (Gen Y). The bottom line is that Gen Y mocks the billable hour and will not spend a career toiling on a billable hour basis. These young professionals have been told they are knowledge workers and that they can work wherever and whenever and need not be fixed to a single location. Consequently, they will work on a flexible and distributed basis, and the clients are insisting that this be offered (nothing new here-this is the secondment model). The critical difference here is that BigLaw loses money on a fixed fee secondment due to the sunk costs associated with the shiny BigLaw offices in the towers. NewLaw will charge less and make money on a secondment because the related expenses are appropriate to the business opportunity.

This is not about "more for less". This is about "different for less". BigLaw will retain its top-of-the-pyramid work (bet the farm litigation, IPO, etc.), but the work that exists within the day-to-day operations (business as usual, i.e. core legal work that repeats with a known frequency) will not remain with the traditional law firm. Others (NewLaw? LPO? Paralegals?) will move in to do the work.

NewLaw is not a revolution that will replace the existing order. This is an evolution in the delivery of legal services that will add another solution to the market in response to client needs (and market demands). I can't imagine a more rational and normal business development

So maybe 'different for less?' But is there the possibility that less is more? The following comment pointed to the need to ask if the accustomed level of legal services is in and of itself really necessary. Like any other business investment, legal services need to generate acceptable, risk-adjusted returns to clients and providers alike. Ron Friedmann (#16)

To achieve legal efficiency and improve value, changing the business model in NewLaw is not enough; lawyers must also change the way they practice law. All the opining about NewLaw trends is speculation; we lack almost any empirical data.

We place too much emphasis on business models and not enough on how lawyers actually practice. **Jordan Furlong** (#13) gets to the latter in his point that 90% of what 90% of law firms do today is the same as it ever was. And that's generous.

Shortly after I began blogging in 2003 I wrote some posts about the need to examine HOW lawyers practice. With legal project management and process mapping, we now see some change. Uptake is, however, slow and requires hand-to-hand combat.

It is not clear to me how many NewLaw organizations actually practice law (or provide "legal support") differently than lawyers and other professionals have always operated. I know of only two organizations – Seyfarth and Novus Law – that have publicly shared details of HOW they work differently.

Irrespective of business model, lower cost and higher value is possible only by changing the way lawyers and other professionals do their work. And efficiency is only one element. Bigger savings likely lie in doing less law. This means making better risk-adjusted decisions about how much to invest in legal services. We talk too much about who does the work and how efficiently. We need to focus more on whether we actually need to do all that work. NewLaw is better equipped to think about that question, but I am not sure NewLaw is doing so much better on that than what I would call OldLaw.

So many of the macro-environmental factors shaping the legal services industry are changing. The next section takes a closer look at some of them. The business management literature is replete with insights into the phenomenon of 'strategic drift'. Among others, the UK's Gerry Johnson in his book Exploring Strategy has shown there is a tendency for organisations' strategies to evolve incrementally on the basis of historical and cultural influences (the so-called 'custom and practice' prevalent in an industry), but eventually this evolution fails to keep pace with the changing environment. It remains to be seen if this is the case in the legal services industry.

ECONOMIC CYCLES

The aftermath of the global financial crisis of 2008 showed once again that law firms and demand for their services are strongly affected by the economic environment. Not surprisingly, the comments reflected little agreement on the current state and direction of the world economy as it affects demand for legal services. **James Edsberg** opined that since the worst of the recession had passed, there is little pressure on BigLaw firms to change their business model. In particular, there was disagreement about whether current problems facing BigLaw firms are cyclical, and therefore transient. **Peter Kalis** argued strongly for the cyclical explanation (see his comment in Chapter 3). Or are the difficulties instead caused more fundamentally by structural changes with the economic cycle overlaid?

My view is that the current green shoots in economies around the world are real, and part of the economic cycle. But, and it's a big but, in my opinion the underlying structural changes in client buying behaviour, substitute activity, breakaway new entrant activity, talent seeking alternative life-career models and price-based competition, mean the downward pressure on BigLaw profitability is inexorable. As it becomes clear profit-per-partner will halve in the next five or so years, one scenario suggests many rainmaking partners will leave BigLaw firms for their own boutiques and fewer top class candidates will come into equity. A negative spiral is in progress.

Growth of the global legal services industry

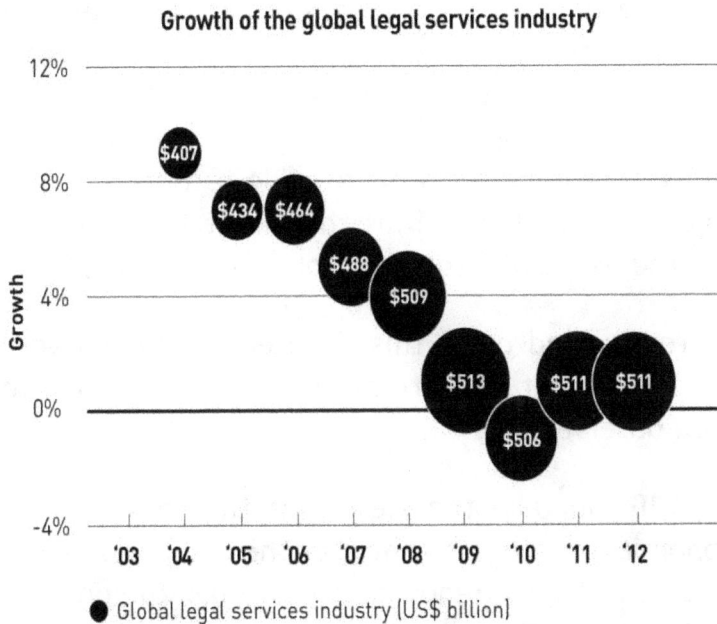

Global legal services industry (US$ billion)

The chart shows the steady slowing of growth in the global legal services industry (defined as fees paid to BigLaw firms) that started in the early 2000s, well before the financial crisis of 2008. While the size of the industry (diameter of the spheres) has grown from ~USD400billion to ~USD500billion, growth has stagnated.

The following comment considered the importance of an assumed and progressive improvement in economic conditions – and a resulting diminution of pressure on all business models.

James Edsberg (#21)

As the economic situation improves, the point of maximum pressure on the law firm business model has passed. Larger law firms can learn from the success of the 'Big 4'. These very large and diversified professional services firms provide a route map for large traditional law firms that want to keep pace with the needs of large and globalising clients.

Where you end up in this debate depends on your viewpoint about the current business climate. I have three observations:

1)   If you take the view that the worst of the economic downturn is behind us then all firms – large and small – have already passed through the point of maximum pressure on their business model – and are out the other side. While a few didn't make it, the overwhelming majority did.

The services sectors in many G20 economies are largely responsible for the recovery and law firms both benefit and make their contribution here. Even law firms in Ireland and Greece are showing signs of recovery. The business environment will continue to get better for all firms. And the result will be that the pressure on them to 'change or die' will weaken.

2)   That said, the ecology of the legal sector will never return to what it was pre-crisis. Everyone recognises that a range of new legal service providers and innovative business models are here to stay.

My impression of talking to large law firm management teams on this issue is that they that they are relatively relaxed that someone is satisfying clients' low margin/ commodity work (e.g. insurance process claims, discovery, contract review, due diligence etc.) leaving them to build value around the complex, high margin matters.

The respectable but low margin work isn't the sort of work which large law's high paid talent likes doing, such firms aren't good at pricing it in conjunction with their high cost base and they haven't always made the process technology investment to deliver it well.

I hear many who say that both these models can coexist happily.

3)   There's nothing that is happening to large legal practices that hasn't already happened in accountancy and consultancy – in fact 'BigLaw' is lucky to have got away with so little disruption until now.

These two disciplines have made room for a variety of providers and niche operators without the business model of incumbents collapsing. The Big 4's business model has barely stumbled despite the deepest global recession since the 1930s. The leaders of 'BigLaw' look at how remarkably resilient the Big 4 are and my guess is that they sleep a little easier at night.

So the economic situation may or may not be placing strong pressures on law firms to change their traditional business model. I discussed the view that the changes are cyclical rather than structural in Chapter 4 in 'Law firms are worrying about the wrong things'. This belief may account for the reluctance of BigLaw firms to take radical action. There was, however, a theme among many commentators that client demands are driving change with the implication that firms will increasingly need to respond.

CLIENTS' BUYING POWER

Clients are questioning BigLaw's reliance on the billable hour as basis for charging. This is causing major pressure on traditional firms, as well as opportunities for NewLaw (and indeed all) firms that adopt a different pricing strategy. Mitch Kowalski (#24)

The changes happening in the legal services industry are structural, not cyclical.

I see structural change in the marketplace. The growth in the number of in-house counsel is structural, not cyclical. This growth is a symptom of law firms pricing themselves out of certain types of work. This never changes back unless firms can demonstrate that they are more cost-effective and provide better value than in-house counsel.

After demanding more for less, GCs don't suddenly say "Hey, charge whatever you want as the crisis is over. "After all, the easiest way for GCs to show a return on investment is to provide evidence of year-over-year legal cost reduction.

As GCs become more comfortable with the Axioms and the Clearspires, the Conduit Laws and the Cognitions and the Gunnercookes, and the AdventBalances, more work will flow to them. Again, this is structural change, not cyclical. After using these firms, GCs will not, absent a bad experience, suddenly give all that work back to traditional law firms.

Will NewLaw get $10B+ deals? Maybe not, but how many $10B+ deals are there out there annually? I am sure NewLaw is quite happy to do 50 $500M deals rather than hoping all year long for that one $10B+ deal. Then factor in that better processes and better technology are designed to allow fewer lawyers to do more work. Global law firms rely on their massive scale to attract work – but what happens when clients realize that the scale is no longer necessary?

The following comment, in addition to discussing changing client demands, touched on BigLaw's vulnerability because of the partnership model and the prevailing basis of partner remuneration systems. Patrick Lamb (#30)

Law firms and in-house law departments are also subject to the business pressures client organisations encounter daily. There will be some winners and many losers among firms in the competition for talent and clients. These forces are generating massive pressure for change, with the outcome being a very different world, now known as the New Normal.

One of the things that struck me is the black versus white, law firm-centric nature of the discussion, and I think those attributes steer the discussion wide of my view. Not to say I'm right, mind you. As someone said, let's circle back together in five years and see how right or wrong all of us were.

First, this discussion, and any discussion of "BigLaw" is, by its nature, focused on firms and businesses that provide service to the corporate world. Little of what we say is applicable in other areas, like family law, consumer law and so forth. That said, some New Law entrants that begin in those areas may find themselves expanding into the more traditional corporate domain.

Second, until relatively recently, legal services in the corporate domain were monolithic–big firms doing work on an hourly basis. There was no belief or expectation that the same forces at work on our clients from a business standpoint would ever apply to law firms. We were, after all, different.

In the past five or so years we have learned that firms and law departments are not immune from these business pressures. We also have learned how fragile firms are. The departure of a few key partners in search of "more" can be enough to cause "a run on the bank." So as firms continue their efforts to grow by hiring market share via aggressive lateral hiring, there will be both winners and losers in the big firm market. The pressures on firms are exacerbated by the competition in the process and content areas that made firms so fat and bloated–document review and research. The pressures from firms like Axiom law cause even more stress on large firms-helping clients bring more work in house where the make versus buy decision rarely cuts in favor of outside lawyers. Again, the added stress load on law firms will cause more to flail and ultimately fail.

We know there will be some number of large firm successes. If nothing else serves to prove the point, we only need look to the accounting world. The numbers in the legal world won't be as limited, but the look will be similar-a relatively low number of hugely successful behemoths and then some relatively successful others, followed by countless small players.

So the pressures from the market are causing changes, as is the growing impact of New Law entrants. The other driver seems to be the clients themselves. More and more clients are realizing they do not need the "IBMs" of the world to handle the vast bulk of their legal work. Most companies never have a "bet-the-company" lawsuit, for example. If they do, there are several worthy behemoths to select from, but the immediate concern of these clients is this year's performance to budget, and they are learning that small firms can provide better service and better outcomes and virtually all of the year in and year out legal work with which businesses grapple.

To me, all of this means that we are moving from a monolithic world to a kaleidoscope environment in which smart and creative people can find new and better models that are much more client-focused in delivering outputs for predictable costs, and clients will be much more sophisticated and savvy buyers, finding suppliers that suit their specific needs. The one size fits all will be a thing of the past.

Another thing that will be a thing of the past is the guaranteed year-in and year-out profits firms have enjoyed. Businesses don't enjoy guaranteed profits every year, so why should we expect law firms to be different? Let's avoid looking at PPP. If businesses could gerrymander their stock price the way law firms play with PPP, there would never be a business whose stock price declined. At some point, the games that allow law firms to show high PPP will have to end, just as the games ultimately ended for Dewey. (Editor's note: Dewey & LeBoeuf LLP is the large New York-based law firm that filed for bankruptcy on 28 May 2012).

The inescapable conclusion is that the market is in the process of an epic upheaval and cleansing. There will be plenty of casualties-in my view, many more than most expect-but one way or another, casualties aplenty. At the same time, huge opportunities exist for the bold.

The next comment was an illustration of increasing awareness of the power of the in-house clients as consumers of legal services. Trish Hyde (#24.1)

In-house counsel have more options than ever before to exercise their buying power.

Clients of the future: Exercise your buying power!

Participating in a recent Beaton Capital forum entitled' Law Firms of the Future', the Australian Corporate Lawyer's Association (ACLA) proposed changing a session title to 'Clients of the Future-Implications for Law Firms' rather than putting it the other way around. The rationale for this is simple.

First, in-house counsel are decision-makers - accountable to the organisation and assessing and assigning workflow based on value and effort.

Secondly, in-house counsel have and are employing more options for managing workflow than ever before: insourcing; up-skilling; project management; and outsourcing to the provider that represents best value – top-tier firms, mid-tier firms, boutique firms, direct briefing barristers, legal process outsourcing and contract labour firms.

Thirdly, in-house counsel are not content with the current situation.

From the 2012 ACLA In-house Counsel Report: Benchmarks and Leading Practices, we know that General Counsel rate their main law firm provider as lacking in aspects of the relationship:

1)   78% agree their main firm provides commercially applicable advice (this means 1 in 5 GCs do not see the advice they receive as commercially applicable)
2)   62% agree their main firm is upfront and transparent about pricing and 57% agree their main firm provides realistic quotes. 2 in 5 GCs do not agree.
3)   46% agree their main firm provides advice at a reasonable price.

Less than half.

4)   21% agree their main firm offers alternate billing methods that work.

ACLA supports the proposition that what really matters in the discussion about the future of legal services is the view of in-house counsel.

The message is not a popular one for law firms as the structure of firms will make change difficult for them – who would vote themselves a pay cut? So the challenge remains on the side of the buyer. Remember, inhouse counsel have the most power to effect lasting change; not just for their organisations, but for their peers and future in-house counsel. Exercise your buying power.

Susan Hackett, whose comment is set out in Chapter 4, similarly referred to widespread discontent among American in-house lawyers about outside legal services.

The focus on large commercial clients in the thread overlooked the opportunities offered by small to medium enterprises (SMEs), as I set out in the following comment. George Beaton (#44.1)

There is evidence of large unmet legal needs among both SMEs and private individuals that could be met through commoditised and cheaper service provision.

British research published earlier this year by the Legal Services Board shows the remarkably small figure of only 16% of SME businesses turning to solicitors for help or advice when faced with a legal problem (see the LegalFutures website piece 'Massive unmet legal need among small businesses').

In the US, the situation seems to be similar-the recently released New York City Bar report 'Developing Legal Careers and Delivering Justice in the 21st Century' discusses the 'persistent unmet legal needs of large portions of the US population'. '[C]ompeting priorities for limited resources [and] a lack of confidence in the value of being represented by counsel' are cited as reasons for Americans not accessing legal services for civil matters (see page 11).

The situation in Australia might be comparable, see for example a 2012 report by Coverdale and others from Deakin University, 'Providing Legal Services to Small Business in Regional Victoria'. The authors found that 55% of the respondent small rural business entities never or almost never, defined as less than once a year, sought legal assistance (see page 1), with utilisation depending on the complexity of the business and the remoteness of the area from rural and regional centres.

The British research shows the reasons why this figure is so staggeringly small. First, the research shows there are many situations where a solicitor could add value to a SME business, but issues with a legal angle are not recognised as such; and are therefore left unattended. In comparison, the Australian report characterises the use of legal services as 'primarily reactive, rather than preventative' (see page 1).

Secondly, where the relevance of the law is acknowledged nine of ten SMEs take action, but the great majority do not turn to a solicitor. Here's the rub. SMEs mostly either handle the problem themselves or seek help from family and friends. Of the minority who do use professional advice, only a third instruct solicitors. In the Australian context, the most frequent source of advice is an accountant (see Coverdale page 1). Translated, this means solicitors become involved in just 12% of the legal problems facing SMEs.

Thirdly, SMEs mostly seek solicitors' help for a narrow range of services. The most common needs are related to employment, intellectual property, and ownership structure. Notably, tax is not seen as legal in nature.

What an opportunity-for solicitors and SMEs! But what are smaller law firms (and by inference law societies) really doing to take advantage of it- for themselves and their potential clients?

Perhaps a better question is 'What is NewLaw doing in the SME and private client space?' The answer is 'Lots'! Since 1994 Epoq in the UK has been developing a range of services using document automation technology with internet delivery. Now there are literally dozens ranging from Rocket Lawyer through LegalZoom to LawyerSelect (see Comment 8 by Greg Carter) and LawPath.

So clients are seeking change, and they are seeking it now. In addition, there might be opportunities through an as yet largely untapped client pool in SMEs. In addition to pressure on the BigLaw business models, changing client demands and new market entrants are providing new opportunities for legal talent.

CAREER EXPECTATIONS

Opportunities for legal talent – and reasons for lawyers to join NewLaw firms – are as diverse as for those firms. There is no doubt the desire for flexibility and a more satisfying work-life-balance will frequently play a role. The following comment echoed John Lennon in envisioning those new possibilities. Greg Carter (#8)

The BigLaw business model relies on leverage for a large portion of its profit. The model is at risk to the extent NewLaw offers attractive alternative careers for lawyers.

Imagine a world where:

1.   Employed lawyers in traditional firms (aka the 'fee-earners') give up the increasingly arduous tournament for partnership (or the daily grind if they weren't in the tournament) and leave to pursue the flexible work/ life balance of viable non-law firm alternatives, including secondment, contract, and crowd-sourcing specialists, or a combination thereof.

2.   Lawyers choose not to enter employment at traditional firms, for the same reasons.

3.   Quality boutique lawyers compete against BigLaw firms, not only on price, but on breadth and depth of expertise, by efficiently forming opportunistic and networked alliances with other lawyers and service providers on a matter-by-matter basis.

1 and 2 are here and rising; 3 is coming and facilitated by LawyerSelect.com.au's "job alliances".

But in practice, what would this look like for careers in law? And what are the many implications for legal educators? The following comment provided some insights. Dan Lear (#33.4)

Young lawyers are interested in new 'virtual' workplaces, but training opportunities are scarce.

I would like to comment on the training issue. I am a lawyer with five years experience who has spent the majority of my career at "NewLaw" firms. I posted about my experiences at such firms, calling particular attention to the training issue, on my <u>Right Brain Law Blog-Growing up virtual</u>.

In summary, my three main observations are:

1) Training is expensive, regardless of firm size-client firms are increasingly unwilling to subsidise it, whether through traditional or NewLaw firms,

2) 'Workplace' camaraderie can develop in a virtual as much as a physical workplace, and

3) Competition on price alone is a losing proposition for NewLaw firms for various reasons.

The training issue will be significant for NewLaw developments. In short, there is a gap and, in my opinion, the growing stratification between BigLaw and NewLaw does not bode well for training new lawyers. Training is very expensive and there seems to be little interest in investing in it.

So the NewLaw job opportunities, while still scarce, might in the future provide many viable career alternatives to BigLaw. The looming problem of a paucity of training opportunities for graduates entering the legal profession is discussed in more detail in Chapter 7.

Eric Lopez suggested graduates might also increasingly seek NewLaw employment opportunities because of the diminishing attraction of BigLaw partnership (comment #42 in the original thread). To maintain competitive profit-per-partner while facing flat or decreasing revenues, firms are making the path to partnership longer and harder as well as reducing the tenure of partners. These trends may be undermining the attraction of partnership for top talent. All this is being compounded by the cultural and economic challenges of the lateral hiring phenomenon.

> **George Beaton**
> @grbeaton_law
>
> "One more time for #BigLaw: Evidence that lateral partner hiring comes at the expense of internal promotions | http://ow.ly/lIgxx"
>
> 6.47am Jun 5, 2013

Today NewLaw firms may be seen as a somewhat risky employment proposition by legal talent. The experience base is far from equal to that in well-established traditional firms. But as **Nicole Bradick** suggested, with the growth of NewLaw services these firms will increasingly become known quantities and will perhaps even become sought after as employers. Nicole Bradick (#33.3.2)

There is concern over the future of training for lawyers if BigLaw continues to contract. NewLaw firms currently rely on BigLaw to train young lawyers and bless them with pedigree. The hope is that NewLaw of the future will train lawyers; when this occurs BigLaw may lose some of its attraction.

A few years in BigLaw does not make one a competent lawyer/rainmaker. I cut my teeth in a mid-sized firm and had significantly more development pressure and experience by the time I "retired" than my BigLaw peers.

Regardless, clients are moved by the BigLaw experience, and countless NewLaw firms use their former BigLaw attorneys as a major selling point.

In my view, that's the result of clients still needing to get comfortable with new models and hearing that a major law firm had previously employed the attorneys gives them a sense of security that they are dealing with a known entity.

My best hypothesis is that over time, being an attorney at certain NewLaw firms will carry enough clout by itself that those firms will start moving away from the marketing message that they have former BigLaw attorneys. When that happens, those firms will feel more comfortable training their own entrepreneurial young lawyers who will only carry NewLaw names on their resumes. My hope is that time will create a sufficiently long history of competent, cost-effective alternatives to BigLaw that those changes will start to really solidify in the minds of clients, who will then start to turn to NewLaw firms because of their reputations and not the reputation of their lawyers' former firms. This should help liberate NewLaw firms to focus on effectively training their own lawyers.

More and more legal talent is seeking work that offers flexibility beyond what BigLaw currently does.

Lawyers might well be willing to forego the resume-building perks and potential for large, albeit delayed, gratification that beckons in a BigLaw career to achieve such flexibility. BigLaw changes aimed at maintaining profit-per-partner might further undermine BigLaw's attractiveness for legal talent. Beyond competing for and through legal talent, firms also compete by using technology to deliver services as excellently and efficiently as possible.

INFORMATION TECHNOLOGY

The importance of sustaining technology for BigLaw and disruptive technology for NewLaw was underscored by the recent article in the American Bar Association Journal, 'Who is eating law firms' lunch?' The article discussed document management services for litigation provided by NewLaw firm Novus Law at costs well below prevailing market rates.

Charles Christian
@ChristianUncut

"@grbeaton_law thanks for the RT. #BigLaw has to know its biz model is cracking under the stress of legacy practices and out-moded thinking"
9.24pm Sep 27, 2012

The next comment posed a relevant question to assess what relevance technological innovations have for NewLaw. Joel Barolsky (#5)

What disruptive technology would an incorporated law firm invest in to become NewLaw and return a healthy profit to investors after Principals were paid?

What's not clear to me is what this technology is that is supposed to be disruptive? What new system or process is going to replace high-level legal analysis, advice and dispute resolution? I can understand more efficient legal processes in discovery and due diligence but to my knowledge, litigation support tools and other process improvement technologies have been used by BigLaw for years. These are mostly sustaining technologies. There are lots of examples of BigLaw partnering with LPOs to reduce costs in legal process work.

Another way to ask this question, assume King & Wood Mallesons incorporated, did an IPO and raised $500 million, what disruptive technology would it invest in to become NewLaw and return a healthy profit to investors after Principals were paid?

If there's no clear and easy answer to my question, then perhaps there is no real disruption going on here and/or there's no need for the new ownership structure and $500m.

Another comment provided examples of uptake by BigLaw of NewLaw technology and services. This shows that relationships between BigLaw and NewLaw might be more complex than simply the survival of the fittest. NewLaw firms can provide necessary support services to BigLaw at lower cost, providing competition but also potentially improving business effectiveness at the same time, subject to clients' buying choices. This is an example of co-opetition in the knowledge economy. Liam Brown (#39)

Well, today, on 31 October 2013, more of BigLaw somewhat started operating according to NewLaw business model principles. LeClairRyan is using UnitedLex's capital and know-how to launch its 400 person Legal Solutions Center. And Seyfarth Shaw announced they are using NeotaLogic's expert systems, document automation and process control technology to improve the efficiency of their lawyers. BigLaw is experimenting.

Joshua Kubicki provided a detailed answer to **Joel Barolsky**'s question about what technology a law firm going public would, could, or should invest in above. Joshua Kubicki (#28)

No lawyer or law firm can change business model without new technologies and processes. Those who want change need to invest in creating, supporting and using new tools. The start-up part of the legal ecosystem is growing because of this.

Joel Barolsky raised the question (in Comment #5) as to what these big technological disruptions are that would enable NewLaw to outcompete BigLaw. I will attempt to answer that question.

We can discuss, debate, and dialogue around business model changes, incumbent tendencies and capabilities for response to change, and new entrants to our hearts' content. In fact, there are far too many conferences and events where this artificial and "feel-good" chatter occurs. A simple inescapable fact is that technology will and is quickening the pace of iteration in legal services. Notice I use "iteration" not disruption or revolution. The legal market is not, has not, and will not be the sole domain of lawyers. Lawyers do not operate in a vacuum with only their lawyer brains – they use tools. The tools of a trade are often a direct reflection of the maturity and capability of that trade. Tools are indeed part of the legal market.. Westlaw and Lexis, providers of legal databases, are players – not that I think they are long for this world. We tend to define legal services far too narrowly and look only inside business models to for innovation and disruption.

As the tools available become more powerful, efficient, and let's use current jargon, 'smart,' so too will the services that the users of the tools provide. And so will the business models. Technology and tools are not just for front-end use but are actually more fundamental to change when employed in the back-end of a business – see data warehousing, logistics platforms, and integrative financial tools. These back-end solutions are what drive pricing, resource management, and delivery flexibility – all key to law firms. If considering what to change a business model – look here first. And where knowledge and communication are essential to a specific business (such as the legal sector) technology is already demonstrating its power to make communication more efficient, accessible and meaningful. Legal is simply catching up.

Axiom is often trotted out as a key indicator of NewLaw's emergence and potential disruption. Where did Axiom spend a large portion of its $28m funding? Technology and tools. It is not so much that Axiom is doing anything new. It hires and provides lawyers to clients. What is new is the "how." And how has Clearspire attempted to differentiate and grow? By investing in technology and tools. Look at the BigLaw players Seyfarth and Littler mentioned earlier. While it is hard to know what exactly these groups are creating and using (for good reason, as it constitutes their competitive advantage) we can look to the external market for signs of meaningful technological disruption (again I am using Joel Barolsky's word here otherwise preferring iteration).

Legal project management software while not sexy or "cool" is becoming a norm in the legal sector. Yes there are still many challenges with getting it into the incumbents' hands, but it is happening and at a greater pace. Mind you this is much different and a heck of a lot more meaningful that taking an LPM CLE or seminar from a consultant. These LPM systems are integrated platforms that cut across task codes, billing, workflow, and resource management. Talk to Axiom and others mentioned above to learn the power these tools hold.

Legal research is also being iterated. We all know that it is harder to bill for research at a firm these days. It is seen as a cost of doing business for firms. While the promise of robust knowledge management systems has not yet prevailed, this has a created a commitment to status quo due to lack of tools, not desire. While research is good for "churn baby churn" billing – with the pullback in client pay-fors – providers are keen to have more powerful tools. Enter the number of start-ups from Neota Logic, Ravel Law, Fastcase, Jurify, Mootus and many others. Do any of these have critical mass yet? Fastcase certainly does and is perhaps the least disruptive/iterative of the bunch. But that is a common trend in technology adoption. Seldom is the most disruptive play the leader in the market initially. I get the sense that Ed Walters at Fastcase knows this and it careful with the scale and frequency of his innovations.

What is perhaps most important about this is that while the incumbents may not have the culture or systems to adopt the new tools rapidly, new entrants are not so constrained. See Alex Hamilton at Radiant.Law. NewLaw has the advantage of being able to test and adopt tools while also building a business model that incorporates them from the get-go.

Legal services are not immune to iteration or disruption; they are merely resistant. The quandary for traditional players is that they are being enveloped by news tools and tech by new entrants, but more so by their clients. When clients begin testing and using new tools, the service provider will be made to use them as well in order to better integrate into their clients' environments. This is happening and will only accelerate. Talk to Westfield Insurance about their approach here. This, I argue, is where the meaningful change is occurring. Perhaps not at the pace some would like but rest assured, technology adoption often looks like a hockey stick – flat at the beginning, then rapid increase in usage.

Technology specifically designed to provide legal information management and process optimisation has the potential to deliver large efficiency increases when integrated into BigLaw work, or as platform for new and stand-alone legal service provision business models. In taking full advantage of technology, NewLaw firms that are not tied to legacy systems and processes might be at an advantage.

enabled the massive growth of firms particularly in the Anglo-American world – and has generated the fabled incomes of the equity partners of BigLaw firms for more than 60 years.

The BigLaw business model was first explained in my post 'Last days of the BigLaw business model'. The following table expands the original definition and summarises the hallmarks of the BigLaw business model as we know it today. The hallmarks are grouped into five categories: Human capital, technology, practice economics, ownership structure and fees.

Categories	Hallmarks of BigLaw	▶ Consequences
Human capital	Attraction and training of top legal talent	High salaries to attract and retain top lawyers
	Lawyers striving to deliver near-perfect technical excellence	Culture of technical excellence at the expense of efficiency
	Lawyers expected to both find and produce work for clients	Lawyer-centric cultures
	Promotion of personal brands of rainmakers	Partner-centricity with firms beholden to partners
Technology	Use of sustaining technologies	Reluctance to use disruptive technology (Innovator's dilemma)
Practice economics	Leveraging full-time lawyers	High fixed costs and the pyramid
	Creation of a tournament to reach partnership	High utilisation of lawyers
Ownership structure	Tight restrictions on the number of equity owners	PPEP is maximised
	Structuring as a partnership	Short-term profit imperatives
Fees	Charge high hourly rates	Clients bear the risk

The NewLaw model, in contrast, is detailed in my post 'How to recognise a NewLaw firm' in Chapter 5. **Bruce MacEwen**, who blogs as Adam Smith, Esq, provided a not-so-faint assessment of law firms that operate on the traditional business model in his 'How much how fast' piece. I quote: The individual lawyer, in cultural terms, is the over-riding unit of organization, not the firm. This is often shamelessly or boastfully cloaked in the rhetoric of "entrepreneurialism," when what it really is, is anarchy.

Our compensation systems revolve around the Sun of billable hours and origination credits of each and every individual lawyer, with hardly any regard to standards of good citizenship, [and] the contribution of everyone in the firm who happens not to be a lawyer, a[lso] k[nown] a[s] nonlawyers, a term I'd like to banish from the earth.

[There is] near-total ignorance about what normal companies call business intelligence, meaning insight into where profitable revenue comes from by practice area, client, attorney, activity, and much more.

And finally our profoundly antique business model of laboring in the trenches as the source of revenue. A friend of mine likes to say that when it comes down to it, lawyers are glorified hourly workers, and that has the distasteful ring of truth.

[...] If law firm leadership needs to alter the ship's course, not everyone can get a vote. In fact, it shouldn't be up for a vote.

The traditional business model to which Bruce MacEwen referred has served law firms and their client very well for a very long time but is now being increasingly challenged for reasons discussed in more detail in Chapter 4. What have long been the many strengths of the BigLaw business model now pose as many problems as possible. In 'The Theory of the Business' Peter Drucker wrote '[s]ome theories of business are so powerful that they last for a long time. But eventually everyone becomes obsolete'. George Beaton (#6) BigLaw might survive, but partner earnings at current levels will not.

I don't under-estimate the resilience of BigLaw owners, i.e. partners. The stakes for them are very high. They are clever and hard-working, as we know. My back-of-envelope figuring indicates the ~2,000 equity partners in the 20 largest firms in Australia earn an average of ~$1m per year (round numbers). Of these I calculate ~1950 would not get a job practising law inhouse for even half this amount. So, in a survival sense, BigLaw is not going to lie down.

But here's the rub. Many of them, perhaps half, could earn more than they do now and more easily in their own boutique law firm. Witness the growing trend to boutiques: White, Ryan, Banki Haddock Fiora, etc. This is back-to-the-cottage and a return to true professionalism for true advisors.

Imagine a world in which there are ten $10B firms (cf the Big4); clients have backward-integrated in

USEFUL SOURCES

Coverdale, Richard, Jordan, Lucinda and du Plessis, Jeane, 'Providing Legal Services to Small Business in Regional Victoria' (Deakin University, 2012) http://www.parliament.vic.gov.au/images/stories/committees/edic/local_economic_initiatives/subs/2A_Providing_Legal_Services_to_Small_Business_in_Regional_Victoria.pdf

Johnson, Gerry, Whittington, Richard and Scholes, Kevan, Exploring Strategy (Financial Times Prentice Hall, 9th ed, 2011)

Lear, Dan, Right Brain Law Blog (1 December 2013) < http://right-brainlaw.blogspot.com.au>

Legal Futures, Legal Futures Blog (1 December 2013)

http://www.legalfutures.co.uk/blog

New York City Bar, Developing legal careers and developing justice in the 21st century (Fall 2013) http://www2.nycbar.org/pdf/developing-legalcareers-and-delivering-justice-in-the-21st-century.pdfNY bar report

CHAPTER 3.
PLAYING BY BIGLAW RULES

The business model that characterises all BigLaw firms is described in this chapter. The BigLaw model has served clients, staff and partners (owners) extraordinarily well for decades. But now the BigLaw business model is encountering many problems in the way it is executed by almost all firms.

Alternatives for delivering commoditised and complex legal services are emerging. One result predicted by Beaton Capital is the severe erosion of partner profits in the not-too-distant future, perhaps to half or less today's levels. At the same time, as the business model that has enabled BigLaw to become the predominant organisational form for the delivery of legal services, it should not be written off.

Peter Kalis saw cyclical, not structural changes, as the cause of the current state of the legal services industry and performance of BigLaw firms. He set out a number of reasons why BigLaw remains willing and able to innovate and continue to provide the best possible client service, particularly in its ability to manage large matters of complexity and critical importance. **John Grimley** pointed to BigLaw's ability not just to react to the demand in the market, but partly to create their own demand. **Joel Barolsky** reiterated a trust in BigLaw's resilience, citing the cyclical nature of changes in the legal industry as well as ongoing innovation such as the use of variable cost structures and fixed-price offers. He also pointed to a shared culture of risk aversion that unites BigLaw and many of their in-house clients. **Jordan Furlong** disagreed with the nature of the observed changes; to him, '[g]rowth is not dead; it has just changed addresses'. He suggested that '[l]aw firms are suffering not from a drop in demand, but from a drop in demand for what they sell, at the price they sell it, in the way that they create and deliver it'. Finally, **Richard Susskind** drew on the self-image of BigLaw partners as doing mostly price-insensitive work, raising the question what would happen if one BigLaw firm started providing these services at a significantly lower price?

BIGLAW BUSINESS MODEL

The BigLaw business model is readily characterised. Based on the professional principles of technical excellence, client-centricity and high standards of ethical behaviour, the model has progressively evolved – starting the 1950s post-World War II – from the practice of law to the business of law.

Let me explain by starting with a little history. In 1819 the firm we know today as Cravath Swaine & Moore LLP was founded in New York. Early in the 20th Century Paul Cravath enunciated the principles of a system to train associates rigorously and promote exclusively from within. To quote the firm's <u>website</u>: "The rotation path fosters collaboration and eliminates the need for associates to compete for work, clients, training or bonuses. The Cravath System places a premium on efficiency and quality of work that no other firm matches, and it was through this value system, which we still use today, that Cravath created a new model for American law firms."

One should add that what Paul Cravath really invented was the foundation for the contemporary BigLaw business model. The modest claim to be "a new model for American law firms" is insufficient. The model rapidly became the basis of the Magic Circle and White Shoe firms of London and the USA – and every other law firm that learned from and copied the model.

In the great industrial boom of the post-World War II era firms seized on the Cravath model and turned it into the BigLaw model. The BigLaw business model property, lending, insurance and similar work types; major projects, e.g. deals and big ticket litigation are 'Hollywood' style productions; industry solutions in work types like trademarks and all manner of private client work are provided by private equity-backed firms; boutiques abound with leverage of 1:1 at most; crowd-sourcing via curated e-marketplaces is prevalent in all legal work types; artificial intelligence and big data analytics are growing rapidly and all back office functions are out-sourced.

This world is upon us. Examples are all around us. The future is here. Does this scenario leave room for high quality domestic and regional firms operating as traditional partnerships? Yes, it does. Of course. BUT what will their partners be earning? Our modelling suggests the answer is a lot less than they are today, perhaps half. The quasi-monopoly rents have been competed away.

James Edsberg (# 21), quoted in Chapter 2, pointed out that there is an assumption among BigLaw firms that their clients' needs for routine, low stakes legal commodity work will be satisfied by other providers. Most of the BigLaw firms have therefore not invested in the technological and labour infrastructure they need to deliver such low-level work efficiently, supplement their mission-critical work and protect their 'under-bellies'. I would add that the examples mentioned by **Liam Brown** (#39) in Chapter 2 – LeClairRyan co-operating with UnitedLex to launch its Legal Solutions Center and Seyfarth Shaw using NeotaLogic's expert systems, document automation and process control technology – are distant from the norm.

So the BigLaw partnership business model, while hugely successful for a long time, is under stress from the inside – structure, culture, etc. – as well as from outside – competition for both the low-end and increasingly the high-end legal work, client price-down pressures, etc.

John Chisholm
@ChisConsult

"RT @grbeaton_law: Will tweaking be sufficient to save #BigLaw firm? NO | ow.ly/dFREh | Or is business model re-invention needed? YES"

8.46am Sep 13, 2012

BIGLAW'S RESILIENCE

Michael Eales
@eales

"Resilience is key in shift from Newtonian to Darwinian business environment. @jordan_law21 @grbeaton_law @AdamSmithEsq bit.ly/TqmQjE"

5.10pm Oct 26, 2012

There is the considerable strength of BigLaw firms that have a history of delivering excellent mission-critical work. **Peter Kalis** commented in a spirited and indomitable manner on the strength of traditional law firms, pondering the state of the world economy, this debate, and the kaleidoscope of firms that is BigLaw. Peter Kalis (#43)

The current state of the legal industry is largely determined by the ebb and flow of the world economy. Far from being uniform, BigLaw is a large, diverse, and competitive industry that continues to innovate. BigLaw provides the advice that clients need to navigate legal complexity due to globalization, regulation and innovation.

1.   Fortunately, because some of the contributors (but certainly not all) are glitterati among the membership of ABLAC, their positions are well known, oft-repeated and require only a quick skim. ABLAC, by the way, is the acronym for AttackBigLaw at Any Cost. ABLACs should not be confused with All Blacks, New Zealand's national rugby union team, who perform a haka before each match. Instead of a Maori challenge delivered from the middle of the playing field, ABLACs tend to stay on the sidelines and say things like, "If I were a player, this is how I would play the game." Their uniforms, unlike those of the All Blacks, seldom require laundering after a match. In fact, the only thing ABLACs have in

common with All Blacks is that they both stomp the ground, albeit for different reasons.

2.   I hate to hide behind my day job again, but if you want to see fuller statements of my views you might try my comment on Professor Hadfield's provocative thesis 'The Hadfield Tunnel: A Comment on Legal Infrastructure and the New Economy'; or my Foreword to Bruce MacEwen's Growth Is Dead: Now What? (2013); or, if you wish to delve into the relationship between law firm structure and client service, my 2011 piece in The American Lawyer entitled "The Grand Illusion." [This point 4 sounds disturbingly close to a famous footnote in American jurisprudence wherein an illustrious professor stated: "See my cogent analysis in …."]

3.   I love conversations like this one because they remind me of my youth. Endless debates in Oxford common rooms the purport of which, in retrospect, was to keep juveniles off the streets and to paralyze them with toxic amounts of caffeine. Or at least I think that was caffeine.

4.   What an egocentric conversation you've spawned! We are all so important. We apparently not only guide our own destinies but also dictate the ebbs and flows of markets. If only the tail that is the legal profession could be made to wag more efficiently or perhaps were to be replaced by an uber-mechanized prosthetic tail of the 21st Century, our dog of a global economy would stop throwing up on the carpet.

It would also help, of course, if the dog were to stop eating roaches, socks and plastic sandwich wraps, but let's focus on the tail and not the dog. In the last week, I read a Bloomberg piece on the paltry bonuses to be handed out on Wall Street this year. Not enough deals apparently. Let's ignore this as we consider the state of BigLaw. A day or two before, I read the New York Times article on the latest Thomson Reuters deal numbers, the basic purport of which was that we're in a 2009-like trough. Let's ignore this as we consider the state of BigLaw. There is a deadly contagion of fecklessness in the political class spreading across the world and casting a paralytic uncertainty over markets. Let's ignore this as we consider the state of BigLaw. Washington is captured by warring camps of ideologues whose political adroitness is roughly comparable to the subtlety of a sledgehammer. Europe is contending with the act of genius that it can maintain 17 different fiscal policies and one currency. Not to worry. Knock, knock. Latvia here. Make that 18 different fiscal policies soon. China, in the age of the internet, apparently thinks it can have a little bit of freedom and a little bit of capitalism but not too much. Good luck with that. Australia has ridden the resources boom engendered by economic expansion elsewhere and now might have actually to tend to its own indigenous economic strengths. Russia, Brazil, India. The beat goes on. Yes, it's all about the legal industry.

5.   The egocentrism of the conversation causes a fundamental question not to be asked, or perhaps I skimmed over it. If the pall of uncertainty were to be lifted incrementally from the global economy, and we were to head, say, in the US toward 3.5% GDP growth, would we even be having this conversation? Is it impossible that we could see that level of economic growth? If you think that is impossible, you're not paying attention to fundamental movements in the energy and manufacturing sectors in the US; to its unmatched level of innovation flowing not only from its great research universities but also from all sectors of the economy, especially but not exclusively the technology sector; and its continuing attraction as a destination for global investments in a troubled world. (In the land of the blind...) Let me put this another way: Last week another managing partner and I depressingly concluded that we are a rolling six months away from — steady yourselves — competing for associates, raising associate salaries and all of the other hoop-jumping that we engaged in pre-2008 because markets will demand the same. Some sea change.

6.   Egocentrism can be an endearing trait — consider those pre-War conversations at Downton Abbey — but when egocentrism is coupled with obliviousness to the darkening clouds over Europe ("In the nightmare of the dark, all the dogs of Europe barked ...." OK, OK. Auden wrote that in 1939, not 1914.) or, in this case, with a stunning lack of insight

into the global marketplace, the egocentrics may be guilty of misleading the young. And I think they are here. Has anyone heard of Reinhart and Rogoff, the authors of This Time Is Different: Eight Centuries of Financial Folly (2009)? Their work has attracted criticism from some other economists — what Americans call "inside baseball" type criticism — but the fundamental point sounds intuitively right: Recessions following financial crises are deeper and longer than those of a more cyclical variety. Economic activity continues to be subdued. Can anyone doubt that this has been true since 2008? If so, may I ask you to look at levels of M&A activity during that period? In the UK, as but one example, 1600 M&A deals involving UK companies in 2007 became 500 in 2009 and that's pretty much where it was in 2012 too. Does the legal industry somehow get a dispensation from such ebbs and flows in the more general economic environment? Is it somehow immune? Of course not. For those who read the legal industry's correspondingly more subdued levels of activity as portending or even reflecting fundamental structural change, radical behavioral modifications, and the end of the world as we know it, my only advice is to buy yourselves some terrific 3-D eyeglasses — perhaps ABLAC can secure a group discount — go to the movie house, and find a real reason to scare the hell out of yourselves.

7.   I also enjoy the way the ABLACs treat BigLaw monolithically. This is a half a trillion dollar global

industry with tens of thousands of organizational actors and millions of individual actors, and the ABLACs treat it like gooey dough that can be pressed into a single shape. Here's a news flash: My law firm competes hammer and tong with other global firms; international firms; Magic Circle firms; Wall Street firms; national firms in dozens of countries; regional firms; super regional firms; boutiques; legal process outsourcers; consultants of all varieties; accounting firms; HR firms; and a variety of other economic actors. We also compete against our clients for the same work, as law departments become more varied, expert and expansive. And we even compete against our own partners who every day of the week take our elevator down and may take someone else's up the next day after, of course, magically reinventing themselves. And we're all in a conspiracy of the dumb!

We apparently don't compete by innovating and becoming more efficient. Primitives, each and every one of us! Recall that scene in Les Miserables. Strapped in place and tugging on cables to pull that boat into dry dock on a stormy day. "Look down, look down. Don't look 'em in the eye. Look down, look down. You're here until you die." Not a Valjean among us. It seems to me that even the most passionate ABLAC must allow for the possibility that we're not really strapped into place and quite as dumb as they fear. Or should I say as dumb as they hope? Could it be — get a grip here — that market forces have shaped us and continue to shape us so that we're meeting the demand curve as it presents itself in the real world. What else would explain the move from pyramidal to cylindrical business models or a variety of other organizational and technological adaptations within the practice of law, including a breathtaking array of alternative fee arrangements and other partnering initiatives with clients? It's probably important that I mention here a crucial distinction between BigLaw and most of the ABLACs: Our mission is to serve clients, not sell books.

8.   May we talk a moment about the global pandemic in Legal Complexity that engulfs our clients? I know that it clashes with the egoistic décor, but let's just for a moment stand in the clients' shoes. Legal Complexity in the 21st Century arises from three principal sources. That is to say, in addition to traditional legal requirements, clients must now contend with legal requirements flowing from globalization, regulation and innovation.

With globalization, we see the movement of people, products, ideas, capital, commodities and services across national borders. As national borders become increasingly less important to commerce, the dictates of sovereign legal systems paradoxically become more important. Clients need advice on this side of the border, on the other side of the border and on how to cross the border efficiently and legally. Law firms can't fake this. And, with respect to NewLaw, whatever that is, good luck if you think you can handle such matters with the sophistication required at all levels. From what I've seen of your qualitative scope, I think BigLaw will probably hold its own.

With regulation, we see the ratchet-like and often inconsistent interventions of governments around the world into private markets. This results not so much from partisan impulse but from burgeoning amounts of knowledge upon which public officials can and must rely when discharging their public duties. We know more now than we did in 2007 about the interdependence of global financial markets. We know more now about the linkage between human behavior and climate change. We know more now about the genesis and progress of sub-clinical disease processes. Public actors must act. We can debate whether they act wisely, but highly sophisticated lawyers are required to address the governmental interface for clients. Is this something NewLaw can address? I guess it could get there some day, but by then it would begin to look a lot like BigLaw.

And by innovation, I mean the creation and protection of intellectual property. It's funny that the ABLACs are prepared to see the end of the world for BigLaw in the midst of an extended deal trough over which it has no control and that all agree will end someday but are unwilling to grant BigLaw's value proposition in IP litigation during the same timeframe. Note to ABLACs: If you wish to throw darts at your computer screen, please click on the following link: <u>Critical Crossroads</u>.

9.   Consider the structure of the legal industry presented on a bar graph where the y axis is 2012 revenue and the x axis is a ranking of the Global 50 law firms. What you see is basically a long, gently sloping tail running from about US$2 Billion to about US$600 Million. Compare that in your mind's eye with the accounting industry where you would see four very high bars on the left side of the graph followed by a sharp decline to the right. The shape of the legal industry, in an era of intense consolidation and globalization, is still up for grabs, unlike the accounting industry. Economic actors compete through innovations in the marketplace and efficiencies gained in their business, not by listening to boo birds perched on the sidelines.

10.   All of us might gain from reading Nicholas Nassim Taleb's latest book, Antifragile: Things That Gain from Disorder (2012). ABLACs give me acute gas attacks because their incessant lecturing from afar violates the basic rule of innovation, as Taleb persuasively sets forth. Innovation doesn't result from a top-down dictate but from tinkering at, in the case of the legal profession, the client interface. Our challenge, as law firm leaders, is to protect our stakeholders both from all of you ABLACs who, like Lincoln Steffens before you, "have seen the future, and it works," and from our own egos when we also

think we know all of the answers. Our job is to propagate a culture of innovation, and let the interplay of creativity and market forces take it from there.

11. Let me holler as loud as I can over to the sidelines in hopes that I can be heard by the ABLACs: As clouds of political uncertainty dissipate, I see an ascending demand curve for legal services that my firm and other BigLaw firms are positioned to address. We intend to compete, and compete hard, for client work based on a value proposition conforming to the needs of a 21st Century clientele and reflecting efficiencies in the delivery of our services. We intend to continue to adapt our value proposition to the real-world legal requirements of clients, to continue to partner with those clients in a variety of ways and to work hard to anticipate the shape of the future demand curve and the preferred modalities for our services in the future. We hope to see some of the ABLACs on the competitive battlefield because, however the battle turns out, clients will be the winners. We're in the business of serving clients, not selling books. But I guess I've already said that.

Peter J. Kalis is Chairman and Global Managing Partner of K&L Gates.

This is the opinion of **Peter Kalis**, an experienced and respected BigLaw leader, on the strength and resilience of BigLaw firms in the face of challenges from outside. All should listen. **Joel Barolsky** similarly refuted any suggestion that current changes predict the end of BigLaw as we know it and agreed that current conditions are the result of cyclical economic, not structural, changes in the market. Joel Barolsky (# 1)

It is clear that the legal market, in Australia and globally, is undergoing significant change. The claim that these changes will mean the end of BigLaw firms and the wholesale replacement by NewLaw is both strategically naive and not backed up by any evidence.

I think many of the commentators underestimate the strength and resilience of BigLaw and overstate the competitiveness of New Law. My view is based on six factors.

1.   Semi-variable cost structures-Law firms are not like manufacturing, retail, airline or mining businesses which have huge, fixed costs. Labour costs typically are around 60% of costs and occupancy 20%. The evidence points to firms being able to scale its workforce up and down with more flexibility than one would traditionally think. While there're some pain, it appears many well-run firms, when needed, are very happy to let redundant people go, de-equitise partners, stop recruiting grads and radically reduce support staff. Similarly, there's been a revolution in workplace design resulting in much more flexible occupancy arrangements. There is little to stop

BigLaw from adopting 'accordion' human capital models, and there's growing evidence that many are, quite successfully.

The latest AFR figures show PPP around $1+ million plus for the top 10 law firms. With relatively flat revenue, this must have come primarily from cost reduction.

2.   Deal-driven profit – cyclical not structural. Last week's Australian Financial Review published a fascinating chart which showed that the number of $10B+ global M&A deals in 2010, 2011 and 2012 combined was less than 2007 alone. This segment of the market drives supernormal profits of the larger BigLaw firms. I think it would be better to wait and see the impact of an increased M&A deal flow on the legal market before calling the end of BigLaw. Frankly, I can't see many clients trusting Axiom and lookalikes with their $10B+ cross-border deals. I think you're drawing structural conclusion from a cyclical change.

3.   Globalisation. Save for Deacons and Phillips Fox, I'd assert that the net impact of all globalisation activity on Australian law firms has been net neutral. While they may have access to more cross-border deals, global clients and better support people, the costs of being part of an international firm are significantly higher than running a purely domestic operation.

A lot of newly global firms operating on discrete profit sharing

models, have by and large the same people, processes and clients. All fleeting benefits accruing have been neutralised by competitors matching their strategy.

4.   Labour arbitrage. Much has been made of the cost differential between Australian and Indian law firms, and the growth of the off-shore LPO market. Mumbai rents are now twice as high than CBD Sydney or Perth. Top talent in India is becoming scarcer and more expensive. All evidence points to the cost differential gap narrowing rapidly.

5.   Fixed pricing and efficiency dividend open to all. You imply that fixed price, capped fee or hard estimate pricing are the privy of NewLaw. Fixed fee pricing has been part of BigLaw for many years. It's just one of many pricing structures they offer their clients. Many BigLaw firms are investing in legal project management and process reengineering. There is very little evidence to assume AFAs will bring down BigLaw, especially that they can play equally in this space, and, in fact, offer clients more choice.

6.   Sow and reap. It seems to me that notwithstanding their ownership structures, the evidence points to some BigLaw firms being willing to invest, to innovate, to sow as well as reap. If partnerships only cared about short-term cash profits

then no firm would have invested in things yielding a long-term return, e.g. IT infrastructure or their brands, or new products/ services, or capability building or... the list goes on. This is clearly not the case!

In another comment (#7), **Barolsky** added that it is not possible to unbundle a large BigLaw firm into its parts and still expect it to be able to deliver work of the same complexity. The relatively small size of today's NewLaw firms therefore precludes them from competing for much of the more complex work done by BigLaw firms. Both **Barolsky** and **Kalis** agreed there is an ongoing need for BigLaw to innovate to meet market demands, and that BigLaw is capable of doing this. They also agreed the complexity of large matters needs the scale and structure of BigLaw firms. **John Persico** (comment #22 in the original thread), while similarly accepting the need for BigLaw for certain complex work, pointed out alternative ways of assembling teams outside a firm structure especially for smaller projects through online marketplaces. Small to medium businesses, rather than large clients, might be more flexible and could lead the way in seeking services through such platforms.

Their large scale might also enable large law firms to take advantage of opportunities that do not exist for smaller, traditional or NewLaw firms, because these BigLaw firms can to some degree actively generate their own demand, as **John Grimley** suggested. John Grimley (#46)

BigLaw has the ability to create demand for its own services.

I would submit that it is a mistake for BigLaw leaders to see their firms as dependent on demand created by clients. Rather, BigLaw can and should create demand for their own services.

BigLaw can do this by deploying teams of (1) highly skilled market research professionals and (2) outbound business developers whose aim is to identify new commercial opportunities for new potential and existing clients. It may come as a surprise to learn that many corporations doing business around the world do not have internal staff capable of identifying these new opportunities. BigLaw can step in and become akin to a central bank or NGO and become a private sector stimulant to the market via the use of a "currency" of proprietary, valuable, actionable market intelligence that will lead to the creation of new transactions by existing or prospective clients.

BigLaw should now be seeking to create transactions and therefore demand for their own services, not reacting to the market by seeing their ability to secure new work dependent on outside economic forces or client-side demand.

Joel Barolsky drew attention to an additional aspect of the relationship between BigLaw and their clients that adds to the resilience of BigLaw in current market conditions. The scepticism and risk-aversion that slows down the uptake of innovative processes and technology in BigLaw firms is mirrored on the client side by in-house counsel who largely have a BigLaw pedigree. Joel Barolsky (#19)

BigLaw's clients are sceptical, risk-averse lawyers with BigLaw pedigrees.

One thing that hasn't got much airplay is the client – their nature, their needs and how they are being met. All the Beaton data I've seen over the past 10 years (George Beaton please update me if I'm wrong) points to Australian clients rating their legal providers around 8 out of 10 on overall performance. This is the highest of all the professions by a statistically significant margin. Even on value for money, notwithstanding the predominance of the billable hour, law firms average around 7.5 out of 10.

By and large, the data suggests BigLaw firms are doing a great job in serving their clients' needs and providing good value. I'm not saying there's no room to get better, but new entrants better beware: the market is being well served by some pretty accomplished providers.

The second aspect that should be recognised that many clients of BigLaw are lawyers themselves.

While you may berate incumbents for lack of innovation, many of their in-house colleagues are of the same breed. Larry Richards, formerly of Altman Weill, published some fascinating data on the personality of lawyers fascinating data on the personality of lawyers. Using a Caliper Profile personality test, Richards' research showed lawyers had "Scepticism" at 90 while the general public were at 50. Lawyers, both in-house and out-house, are in the main conservative and risk averse. If one accepts this then my thesis is that the NewLaw diffusion curve is going to be a lot longer than one might initially think. Clearly, there are some early adopters on the client side, but my observation is that it's still slow going. One illustration of this is recent Hildebrandt data that shows AFA growth being flat despite all the hype.

Warren Riddell points out we're in a buyers' market. Well, of course we are. In fact, we've been in one since 2008. Yet despite five years of benign market conditions, we're still seeing the top end of BigLaw delivering $1m+ profits to its equity holders. On top of this, about two-thirds of these firms have had to deal with major merger and integration distractions.

There's nothing that been written in this thread that changes my opening line: "I think you underestimate the strength and resilience of BigLaw and overstate the competitiveness of NewLaw".

Joel Barolsky concurred BigLaw's resilience will be sufficient for its firms to innovate as necessary. This is because client demands are unlikely to change more quickly than BigLaw can adapt, given the shared sceptical and risk-averse BigLaw culture that exists between provider and client. This opinion was not held by the proponents of the impact of changing buying behaviour by clients, as discussed in Chapter 1.

Jordan Furlong took a closer look at what BigLaw innovation would mean, given certain structural characteristics of BigLaw, and pointed out that while firms at the top end of the market will benefit from their strong brands, they still face challenges that go to the very core of their existence. Jordan Furlong (#13)

Large law firms are facing a near-complete transformation of their business models and are mostly ill-equipped to see this process through. Large firm associate training is designed to produce law firm employees, not entrepreneurial lawyers of the future.

A few more observations from your northern Commonwealth cousins:

1)   I don't think anyone is seriously asserting that demand for high quality, high-stakes legal service will collapse, and that large full-service firms will go with it. If anything, I expect that demand will grow —

correct me if I'm wrong, but I don't think demand for legal services has ever shrunk or even plateaued on a year-over-year basis since we started measuring it.

But it's important that we understand this: demand for legal services is not the same thing as demand for lawyers in law firms. The flat-lining or decline in law firm profits sharply contrasts with the continuous growth of all the NewLaw firms we've been discussing. Growth is not dead — it's just changed addresses. Law firms are suffering not from a drop in demand, but from a drop in demand for what they sell, at the price they sell it, in the way that they create and deliver it.

2)   Joel Barolsky has pointed out, rightly enough, that the top BigLaw firms are doing more than fine, and that many BigLaw firms see what's happening and are taking steps to address it. Two points here.

First, the elite members of BigLaw, as is the case with the elite members of any group, will ultimately be fine. If I were a member of an AmLaw 10 firm, I would obviously be very interested in what's happening to the market, but I wouldn't be panicked: my firm's brand is more than strong enough to survive the current crisis and, more importantly, survive the gradual but inevitable process of change that's coming our way.

But if I were in a firm from AmLaw 11-200, I would be concerned, and as I go down that list, my concern would edge into panic. These firms are like houses of cards, impressive to look at from the outside but extremely vulnerable and structurally unsound at their core. They may survive the crisis — most are stumbling through alright — but I don't see them surviving the change process that's to come. More on that in a moment.

Second, it's one thing to say law firms are aware of their challenges; it's entirely another to say that they can actually do something to address them. For all the talk about change in law firms, very few existing firms have actually changed the way they do business, the way they create, carry out, deliver and price their services. Among large North American firms, I can name Littler and Seyfarth, and that's it.

Some firms implement LPM, but in hardly any firm is LPM close to being standard operating procedure across every or even most departments. Technology is utilized to organize information, but not to carry out otherwise billable tasks. No existing law firm makes fixed-fee pricing their default method, and those firms that do sell flat-fee services on some files cannot guarantee they're turning a profit on same. 90% of law firms are 90% identical today, in terms of how they run their businesses, as they were 20 years ago.

3) The challenge facing law firms, as I said before, is not surviving this crisis: most firms have enough size, momentum and market share to run this gauntlet,

although they will certainly be damaged in the process. The real challenge lies in recognizing that a new environment for the purchase and sale of legal services is rapidly developing, meaning that the old ways of doing business no longer interest the market and that new ways of doing business will be required. Most law firms have at least the five following challenges lying between them and that goal:

a)   The fundamental supremacy, in cultural terms, of the individual lawyer over the firm (rather than the reverse, as in, say, accounting firms).

b)   The focus on full-time lawyer effort as the dominant source of productivity and revenue (rather than on systems, technology, and those who are not lawyers).

c)   The near-complete lack of comprehensive business intelligence about the firm's inventory, costs of delivering service, true productivity (rather than "hours billed," which is a ludicrous metric), and true profitability of files, clients, and the firm in general.

d)   The compensation principle that lawyers are to be rewarded almost 100% on the basis of business originated and time billed to client files (rather than, say, management, training, client relations, publishing, marketing, community work, etc.), and that such compensation is to be paid out by draining annual profits in full every year.

e)   The near-complete absence of succession planning and its antecedent, true partner development and mentoring (this is what will end up

94

killing most firms: they will die with the passing of their most important rainmakers who have never considered it to be in their interests to share relationships with key clients).

Most firms would struggle mightily to change any one of these states of affairs; in reality, they need to solve all five of them. My fundamental concern is that even if a firm turned itself, with all effort and goodwill, to this challenge, it would still be beyond most firms to accomplish, because the five elements I listed above aren't just "features" of the firm — they're inherent characteristics, sunk deep into the firm's originating baseline DNA.

So, to make a long story short (too late), I share George Beaton's real concern for the medium-term future of many law firms. Like I said, I don't think it's necessarily this current downturn that's the major issue; it's that this downturn is effecting and ushering in a new set of market conditions that make the environment essentially unsuitable for the traditional law firm business model, and that most firms lack the wherewithal to adjust to the new environment without tearing themselves apart in the process.

The following comment from the coalface by **Richard Susskind** illustrated the view that many BigLaw partners seem to hold - the services of their firms are mostly complex and price-insensitive because of their mission critical nature. Richard Susskind (#26)

I am currently at the 18th Law Firm Leaders' Forum in New York. I gave the opening talk, setting out the thinking in my latest book, Tomorrow's Lawyers. Three panelists were asked to respond. They are leaders of first rate firms. They did not speak with one voice but there was a sense from two of the three that the disruptions that George Beaton and I discuss will not extend into the best firms who undertake the most complex work – work, that they argued, is price insensitive. As I said in reply, and echoing, in fairness, one of the panelists, that category of price insensitive work is diminishing. More than this, I suggested that if one leading law firm breaks rank and delivers world-class service at significantly lower cost, using alternative methods of sourcing, then the market will change irreversibly.

This comment took us from BigLaw's resilience back to the nature of disruptive innovation discussed in Chapter 1. Susskind's comment suggested the inevitable innovation by BigLaw might itself become the trigger for far reaching market changes.

USEFUL SOURCES

Beaton, George, 'Last days of the BigLaw business model' on Beaton Capital,
Bigger. Better. Both? (6 September 2013) http://www.beatoncapital.com/ 2013/09/last-days-biglaw-business-model/

Drucker, Peter F 'The theory of the Business' (September 1994) Harvard Business Review Magazine http://hbr.org/1994/09/the-theory-of-thebusiness/ar/1

Hopkins, Kandy, 'Flat AFA Growth Rates May Not Tell Whole Story' on Hildebrandt Institute, Hildebrandt Blog (October 10, 2013) http://hildebrandtblog.com/2013/10/10/flat-afa-growth-rates-may-nottell-whole-story/

Kalis, Peter, 'Critical Crossroads' http://www.youtube.com/watch?v=7L_OLQFATKo

Kalis, Peter 'The Hadfield Tunnel: A Comment on Legal Infrastructure and the New Economy ' (2012) 8(1) I/S: A Journal of Law and Policy for the Information Society http://moritzlaw.osu.edu/students/groups/is/files/2012/02/Kalis.pdf

MacEwen, Bruce, 'How much how fast' Adam Smith Esq Blog (October 25, 2013) http://www.adamsmithesq.com/2013/10/how-much-how-fast/

MacEwen, Bruce, Growth Is Dead: Now What? (Adam Smith Esq, 2012)

Reinhart, Carmen M and Rogoff, Kenneth S, This Time is Different: Eight Centuries of Financial Folly (Princeton University Press, 2009)

Richard, Larry 'Herding Cats: The Lawyer Personality Revealed' *Report to* Legal Management 29(11), August 2002
http://www.managingpartnerforum.org/tasks/sites/mpf/assets/image/MPF%20-%20WEBSITE%20-%20ARTICLE%20-%20Herding%20Cats%20%20Richards1.pdf

Susskind, Richard E, Tomorrow's Lawyers-An Introduction to Your Future (Oxford University Press, 2013)

Taleb, Nassim Nicholas, Antifragile: Things that gain from Disorder (Random House, 2012)

CHAPTER 4.
BIGLAW'S CHALLENGES

Having reviewed the strength and resilience of the BigLaw model, I now turn to the challenges that are confronting firms based on this model. One key problem might be a lack of awareness among the decision-makers of the perfect storm BigLaw is facing, as outlined in my next comment. This assessment is supported by **Mitch Kowalski**, who pointed out that BigLaw firms are not keen to compete for less complex work, and **Derek Minus** who also noted such a lack of awareness particularly in Australia.

Adding to all this is a common trait of risk aversion among lawyers that is probably delaying the uptake of new technology, processes and business models. It might also be hindering an analysis of what level of legal services is truly necessary as a matter of business efficiency, rather than desirable from the provider's point of view.

Ken Jagger and **Patrick Lamb** both saw partnership structure as a, perhaps the, significant obstacle to BigLaw firms making changes in the way that they do business, because it leads to a focus on short-term profits and little true long-term investment in sustainable business practices. Historic and current profit levels are not sustainable in BigLaw firms. Beaton Capital's analysis indicates that for BigLaw firms based on business as usual, profit-per-partner will halve within ten years. A recent article by William (Bill) D. Henderson presented data showing an increase in BigLaw leverage that suggests continuing short-term profit orientation. **Eva Bruch** foresaw a drastic reduction not just in profitability, but also in the number of BigLaw firms.

Beyond the challenges from within because of the partnership structure, BigLaw firms are facing increasing competition – and declining demand – from in-house legal departments. **Mitch Kowalski** viewed this as a structural change in the market. **Susan Hackett** posited that in spite of long-standing relationships, in-house counsel will be more than willing to acquire services from entities other than BigLaw firms given the right price incentives. For secondment services, NewLaw firms with their lower overheads and labour flexibility can provide such incentives, as **Peter Carayiannis** affirmed. And **Karl**

Chapman foreshadowed that there will be long-term competition through outsourcers using innovative processes to provide legal services more efficiently than even in-house legal departments can.

The efforts by BigLaw firms to address (some of) the issues were discussed. **Ken Jagger** saw an increasing awareness among BigLaw firms of the challenges raised here. **Liam Brown** cited examples of BigLaw-NewLaw co-operation. But given the many simultaneous pressures from within and without that BigLaw firms are facing, all change will be hard, and it seems likely many BigLaw firms will not be able to respond adequately. But some will succeed.

LACK OF CONCERN

George Beaton: 'Law firms are worrying about the wrong things'.

Technology is a key driver of change in the legal services industry, but so are alternative business models and their ownership structures, enabled by new legislation, as is occurring in the UK. Legal commodity work delivered using sophisticated technology can be profitable for external investors.

More than 500 people gathered at the LawTech Futures conference in London in April 2013 and concluded that most law firms are worrying about the wrong things. The key take-out, in a sentence, was that no one with a blank sheet of paper would design a law firm like those we know today. Headline-catching, yes. Exaggeration, no. The rapidly converging trends now in progress make it certain that external and internal forces will change the way firms are configured to serve clients, the profits they make and the way people work in them.

There were very few nerds and their acolytes amongst the speakers, panelists and audience. Some seriously heavy-hitting law firm leaders were there to learn and share ideas. And learn we all did. This wasn't an IT or a technology conference, even though ITC and related vendors were there in droves because technology is a big part of the future and an enabler, at times a driver, of change. Rather, LawTech

Futures was focused on clients' needs and the strategic options, future shape, governance and prosperity prospects of law firms.

The LawTechFutures conference showed in graphic detail just how much change is occurring. As one might expect, dramatic references were made to the impact of similar changes in music, books, news and IT. The real point is what's driving the revolutions in these disparate industries is now doing the same in others such as health care, education, advertising and real estate. And it's going to be law's turn next.

The biggest single change is the introduction of alternative business structure (ABS) legislation in the

UK. This makes possible the external ownership of law firms. In only two months since its introduction there have been more than 200 applications to the regulator. I hear some say, it's all very well for Slater & Gordon to be able to extend its acquisitions into the UK, but what's it got to do with us? The answer is 'Lots'. Not because large corporate law firms are going to sell partially or fully to investors. Rather because a large chunk of the commodity work done by these firms–as much as 70% in some cases–will be taken away by much more efficient providers using technology and funded by private equity and other investors hungry for this new asset class. And not just LPOs in India and elsewhere, but by so-called non-firm firms such as Axiom and Advent, IT vendors and others.

External ownership has been possible in Australian law firms for many years, but little innovation has occurred because of our continuing benign economic conditions. Not so in the UK, which others all around the world are watching. America is stirring–and change will come. The avalanche has begun because entrepreneurs see the fallibility of the traditional law firm business model and know the profits to be made. Disaggregation of legal services is nearly a decade old and still only has a 1% share of the global market. So why should large law firms worry about Pangea3 and other the hundreds of other LPOs, and Axiom, Advent, Clearspire and their many imitators?

The answer is because these are innovators and early adopters in the new ways. They have taken the risk, proven the concepts and in many cases already provided handsome returns to their private equity backers, witness the purchase of Pangea3 by Thomson Reuters. Now more are following, with even deeper pockets, to invest in scale and sophisticated technology. As Tom Peters once aptly put it, danger lurks in that slither of the pie chart marked 'Other'. How true in the legal sector.

We are also about to see another form of disaggregation, this time adversely affecting the advisory crown jewels of the large law firms. Specialist boutiques ranging in size from a handful of partners to maybe 20 or 30 will form de novo or by breakaway from large firms. This is not new; there are already dozens of small specialist law firms dominating niches as diverse as inbound Chinese investment, IP and hotels. What will be new is the size, quality, business model and global network of these firms. Many will be high-end corporate advisory firms.

And in many ways they will be virtual. They will outsource their back offices entirely. They will compete with the top tier pure domestic and global firms and they will be exclusive members of a network of like firms in key countries. Will they be able to compete successfully for all the 'bet-the-company' work done by large firms? No, but they will take large chunks and make eye-watering profit margins in the process.

It's noteworthy what this post has not specifically addressed: globalisation, consolidation, business process re-engineering, crowdsourcing, much greater mobility and talent, to name a few. All these, and more, are inter-linked with those mega trends I have covered: deregulation, innovation and disaggregation. The most exhilarating aspect of all the trends is their velocity. As the late Steve Jobs once stated, you can't connect the dots looking forward; you can only connect them looking backwards.

No firm has time to 'wait and see what's going to happen'. Every firm is being affected, now. It's time to understand and act. Many law firm leaders are worrying about the wrong things. Opportunities and dangers lie in places of which most are not yet aware.

George Beaton
@grbeaton_law

".@AdamSmithEsq on dearth of real innovation in #BigLaw | ow.ly/28bJKi | Who, other than #NewLaw, has defined 'innovation'?"

7.47am 29 Nov 2013

As **Richard Susskind**'s comment in Chapter 3 illustrated, there is a common conception among law firm leaders that while changes are occurring, their complex, mission-critical work will not be much affected. Unfortunately, there were few comments from BigLaw firms in this conversation with the result this belief has not been well ventilated here. More comments from this quarter would have provided a more detailed view of how BigLaw is thinking and how BigLaw believes firms will be affected by the changes around them. The exception is the comment by **Peter Kalis** in Chapter 3.

George Beaton
@grbeaton_law

"@richardsusskind says 'It was ever thus. Law firm leaders are very slow to respond online' | Clearly true, but all are deprived in the discussion"

8.38am Oct 4, 2013

A view that BigLaw firms will be able to continue to operate on their traditional model doing complex work overlooks the fact that they depend on their lower-end work to a very considerable degree to hold clients and generate profit. Mitch Kowalski (#24)

[...] But Global firms should not be patting themselves on the back too quickly. As we know,

Global law firms need to do "everyday work" to keep their troops busy between the "bet the firm" work. As a former Baker partner, I can tell you that most work done at my office and in most Baker officers is not complex "bet the firm" work. It was generic corporate deals, generic securities work, generic litigation, generic real estate.

Global firms are not at all well positioned to compete for that "every day" work. If they lose it, they are in trouble. As NewLaw eats away at "every day" work, Global firms will have greater difficulty keeping their troops busy between the "bet the firm work." [...]

The theme of lawyers, in Australia and overseas, not seeing the changes around them as affecting them continued. Derek Minus (# 2)

Australian lawyers see changes as an 'overseas thing'.

What **George Beaton** writes about the changes in the legal services industry resonates with my sense of business and societal change being driven by communications and IT. Although I have been practising as a barrister for the past 20 years, I spent my first 20 years as an employee working for US and UK multinationals in marketing and business development.

It is fascinating to see some sectors in turmoil. For example, I have done work over the past few years in retail leasing disputes and training. And with NSW farmers and producers in horticulture who are searching for ways to get back into the game. So many big firms are reeling from the change in their margins.

But the Australian lawyers I talk with seem too unconcerned, aware of "overseas changes" but not unduly worried about continuing to do what they have always been doing. I think that is a mistake, things are changing, maybe slowly now but inevitably.

So there seems to be a lack of awareness among BigLaw decision-makers about the nature and magnitude of the changes going on in the legal services industry.

George Beaton
@grbeaton_law

"Do #BigLaw firms think they can't be substituted? | Legal IT Insider ow.ly/20uLGP"

8.10am Jul 7, 2013

If this situation does not change, it will delay or prevent BigLaw firms from modifying their business models to respond to these trends.

RISK AVERSION

Joel Barolsky (#19) in Chapter 3 characterised lawyers as both sceptical and risk-averse. These traits probably delay the ability of both BigLaw and in-house counsel to take up new business models and ideas, no matter how beneficial. For a discussion on how these risk-averse views change through in-house socialisation to fit in with business rather than legal norms, see **Susan Hackett** (#34) below. This, in conjunction with a lack of awareness or a reluctance to acknowledge disruptive change, is further limiting BigLaw's ability to respond effectively.

It might also prevent a dispassionate analysis of what levels of legal services are ultimately necessary to manage client business risks as proposed by **Ron Friedmann** (#16) in Chapter 2.

Irrespective of business model, lower cost and higher value is possible only by changing the way lawyers and other professionals do their work. And efficiency is only one element. Bigger savings likely lie in doing less law. This means making better risk-adjusted decisions about how much to invest in legal services. We talk too much about who does the work and how efficiently. We need to focus more on whether we actually need to do all that work.

PARTNERSHIP STRUCTURE

Partnership structure is an important hallmark of the BigLaw business model. But as was pointed out frequently in this thread, the partnership structure makes fundamental change problematic. **Ken Jagger** (a former BigLaw partner himself) summed up the difficulties caused by the partnership model:

For me though, the main impediment remains the ownership structure. Their leadership may see the need to retain profits, raise capital, establish new business lines and restructure but convincing large groups of partners with a short term focus is problematic. At best it slows the process down, at worst it stops innovation dead.

Addressing this conundrum, **Bruce MacEwen** succinctly quipped 'If law firm leadership needs to alter the ship's course, not everyone can get a vote. In fact, it shouldn't be up for a vote.'

Jordan Furlong in Chapter 3 (#13) pointed out problems with the partnership model in more detail – the cultural supremacy of the individual lawyer over the firm, compensation based on billable hours, annual distribution of (nearly) all profit, as well as the lack of effective succession management and mentoring that stem from this.

And there is the vulnerability of the BigLaw firm that is a collective of key partners, or as Americans describe it, a 'hotel for lawyers'. Faced with the same business pressures as their clients, partners can damage the viability of their firms by taking their client portfolios elsewhere if they are concerned about decreasing profitability, as **Patrick Lamb** (#30) detailed. Patrick Lamb (#30)

[...] In the past five or so years we have learned that firms and law departments are not immune from these business pressures. We also have learned how fragile firms are. The departure of a few key partners in search of "more" can be enough to cause "a run on the bank." So as firms continue their efforts to grow by hiring market share via aggressive lateral hiring, there will be both winners and losers in the big firm market. The pressures on firms are exacerbated by the competition in the process and content areas that made firms so fat and bloated–document review and research. The pressures from firms like Axiom law cause even more stress on large firms-helping clients bring more work in house where the make versus buy decision rarely cuts in favor of outside lawyers. Again, the added stress load on law firms will cause more to flail and ultimately fail. [...]

George Beaton
@grbeaton_law

"#BigLaw PPEP levels are doomed without re-invention http://ow.ly/rfDEB"

6.21pm Sep 5, 2013

Beaton Capital's analysis indicates that partner profits are likely to decrease drastically if business as usual continues.

PPEP levels are doomed without re-invention

If business is continued as usual, PPEP levels will halve in less than 10 years.

If **Bruce's MacEwen**'s recent analysis of the historical trend in revenue, demand and realization doesn't worry you as an owner of a BigLaw firm, then don't read any further. Beaton Capital has modeled a forward look at the drivers of BigLaw PPEP, profit per equity partner or equity point. The picture isn't pretty. Adam Smith Esq, **Bruce MacEwen**'s blog name, delivers a robust microeconomics 101 tutorial to BigLaw in a recent post ominously titled 'Growth is Dead: Part 1'. The early paragraphs make scary reading: "If you want to deny things have changed, you would point to Equity Partner Rates and PPEP, but for purposes of this discussion I disagree. The time series I would call out are Revenue, Demand and Realization – all down. I focus on those three series because equity partner rates and PPEP are internal financial reports essentially under the control of firms (at least in the short run, and three years still qualifies as the short run). The ones I prefer to focus on are creatures of the market and reflect market forces."

Bruce draws on the Hildebrandt/Citibank time series, which by definition is based on actual historical data for a substantial sample of large US law firms. A ray of hope appears to lie in the economic variables under the control of law firms – charge out rates and equity points on issue. These indicators are still tracking in positive territory for law firm proprietors. Any hope is, however, dashed by making some basic assumptions, all grounded in well-documented trends in market forces, and applying these assumptions to a 10-year forecast of what will happen to PPEP in a steady state law firm. Let's face it, as I have argued elsewhere almost all large law firms are practising in a business-as-usual way.

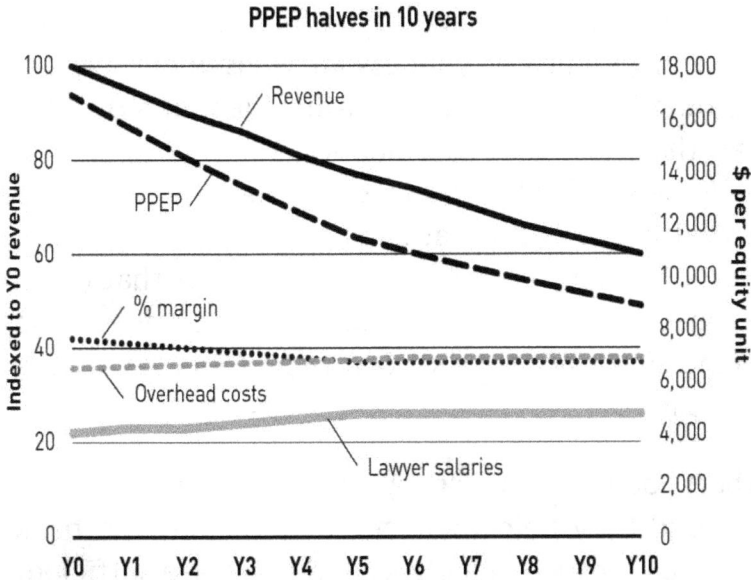

PPEP halves in 10 years

In the chart we have modeled a firm starting with annual revenue of $100 million and 2,500 equity points on issue. Then we assume revenue decreases at 5% each year, lawyer salaries increase 3% annually for five years (and then stabilise), other overhead costs increase 1% per year for five years (and then also stabilise) and, finally, this firm holds its equity points at 2,500 for each of the 10 years. Here's the result: PPEP halves in less than 10 years.

Now you might want to argue no firm will make such small adjustments for this long. Surely, you might say, this firm will further cut staff and reduce space and also reduce the points on issue and/or cut the number of equity partners. Partners accustomed to incomes of these levels are not going to be passive in the face of a decline of this magnitude. Yes, of course rational business owners will do these things. And the result, depending on your assumptions of how rapidly and decisively the firm acts, will be less of a disaster than the chart suggests. But will this fictitious firm really be quick off the mark and decisive? We know several firms that are already on this slippery slope. These firms are not acting in any manner that could be described as strategic and decisive. The partnerships are stuck. Some partners deny the forecast.

Others believe the 'good old days' will return–provided they hold their nerve. After all, the bank hasn't coming knocking yet. And there are sufficient senior associates in the ranks signaling an interest in becoming equity partners.

Law firms need to make up their own minds about the future and how their business models need to change to ensure they can continue to serve their clients and prosper at the same time.

So there are problems with the partnership structure. The question is, how much of a threat to the BigLaw business model do these problems pose? A forthcoming article by William D. Henderson in the International Review of Law and Economics, 'From Big Law to Lean Law', indicates the answer is probably a huge one. Henderson discusses Larry Ribstein's 2010 essay 'The Death of Big Law' and supports Ribstein's predictions with more recent data. He demonstrates that the ratio of other lawyers to equity partners in the US has increased by more than 50 % from 1994-2012 (Fig 3), drawing 'into sharp relief the tendency of Big Law to use its existing reputational capital to maximise short-term profits rather than take the steps necessary to build a stronger organization capable of taking market share from competitors'. And as an illustration of the shift in the provision of legal services overall, Henderson showed that while the number of employees in law firms has only increased by about 10 % since 1999, the number of employees employed by 'other' legal services has risen by 140 % (Fig 6).

George Beaton
@grbeaton_law

"#BigLaw 'culture of short-termism is widespread and deep' concludes Stephen J Harper | http://t.co/UFHzIwxxxm | Can anyone see a solution?"

2.45pm Jun 6, 2013

Mike Ayotte (comment #31 in original thread) agreed with the forecast of a large decline in partner profits. He based this on a calculation detailed in his post 'What clients want and why BigLaw can't deliver' on his blog, The Last Honest Lawyer. He reached the conclusion that at this point, the work that used to be done by associates is offered for less than the fixed cost of an associate's salary (let alone the substantial overhead) by firms.

Eva Bruch anticipates that the ongoing changes will lead to a clear decrease in the number of BigLaw firms. Eva Bruch (#38)

One of the brakes for innovation in the legal sector is in its own DNA: law firms are professional ones ruled by partnership systems such as the "eat what you kill" model that promote the individual economic interests of each partner to the detriment of the common good. The road to innovation includes managing this reality.

Ron Friedmann rightly points out that we know very little about how these new business models (NewLaw) work and draws attention to the lack of reliable data on the sector. Meanwhile, **Alex Hamilton** of Radiant Law does provide some of that know-how, explaining that their business model is based on LPO, fixed-fees and 'experimenting' with new technologies in search of creative solutions to common problems in legal services delivery. I think **Alex** has pinpointed where NewLaw is gaining its true competitive advantage.

BigLaw is also investing in new technologies; some of the biggest Spanish firms are certainly doing so. But it is also true that many lawyers in these firms see these innovations as more work for them, as more time-consuming, rather than as the opportunity to create a better practice and a stronger business.

At this point, I agree with **Ken Jagger**, among others, when he suggests some aspects of ownership structure are a big impediment to innovation. Remuneration models like 'eat what you kill' have a short-term focus in that they penalize investment in technology, research and management. This type of system may help reduce fixed costs, but they also limit a firm's ability to adapt to the market.

In my opinion the BigLaw model is not going to disappear altogether. There is – and will always be – a (small?) part of the community that values their expertise and the intangible benefits of their brands, as **Richard Susskind** has noted.

But I also think traditional firms as we know them today will be halved in number in just a few years. Innovation in processes, technology, commoditization and LPM will make the business of legal services more industrialised. And document automation, online platforms and virtualization will do the rest.

In conclusion, the partnership structure poses significant threats to the BigLaw business model. By emphasising short-term profit over longer-term strategies and striving for high prices to preserve margins in the absence of a defensible business model, BigLaw firms are being slow to make changes and are vulnerable to desertion by key rainmakers.

COMPETITION FROM IN-HOUSE COUNSEL

Mitch Kowalski (#24) characterised the changing role of in-house counsel in the legal services marketplace thus...

The growth in the number of in-house counsel is structural, not cyclical. This growth is a symptom of law firms pricing themselves out of certain types of work. This never changes back unless firms can demonstrate that they are more cost-effective and provide better value than in-house counsel.

And there is a growing realisation of their own bargaining power and freedom of choice among in-house counsel, as evidenced by **Trish Hyde**'s comment (#24.2). Trish is CEO of the Australian Corporate Lawyers' Association (ACLA).

In-house counsel have employed and are employing more options for managing workflow than ever before: insourcing; up-skilling; project management; and outsourcing to the provider that represents best value – top-tier firms, mid-tier firms, boutique firms, direct briefing barristers, legal process outsourcing and contract labour firms.

Ron Friedmann (comment #37 in original thread) pointed to a lack of data on the quantity of legal work done in-house compared to work done by law firms. The growth in ACLA membership reflecting the increasing number of in-house counsel may be a useful proxy at least for Australia.

Membership, while of course not mandatory for in-house counsel, has been growing at a 7% compound annual growth rate from 1998 to 2013.

For the US American market, Clayton Christensen assumes in his recent article 'Consulting on the cusp of disruption' that one third of the work in the USD 500billion US legal market is performed by in-house counsel. **Joel Barolsky** (#19, Chapter 3) asserted in-house counsel, risk-averse like the lawyers at the BigLaw firms, will not lightly abandon their business relationships with those firms, and will not easily shed their accustomed ways of practising law. **Susan Hackett** refuted this by pointing out that all that is needed for in-house lawyers to desert providers they are not satisfied with is 'time and the proper in-house incubator for a recovering outside counsel to be reborn as a savvy in-house client'. Susan Hackett (#34)

While it is critical to focus our attention on the changing NewLaw firm business model, it is equally critical to remain grounded in developing solutions that are aligned with client needs and perspectives. In this exchange, Susan reminds us that law firms who confuse clients who have always sent them business with clients who are satisfied with the work are making a dangerous assumption.

My experience is almost totally on the client side – as the GC of the Association of Corporate Counsel for more than 20 years, and as a longtime advocate (and grenade-thrower) in the "NewLaw" brand of conversation for most of that time, here's what I would add to the stew: just because an in-house lawyer continues to send work to a law firm or relationship partner, even one with whom she's worked for many years, doesn't mean she's satisfied with the service. And just because she scores a law firm as an 8 or 9 or 10 when asked to complete the evaluation about a firm that (beloved or not) she feels she must continue to use (and therefore must validate), doesn't mean she wouldn't drop them in a New York Minute if something better came along that provides her similar "quality" AND superior efficiency: in cost control, knowledge practices, process re-engineering, and better trained staffing.

Every year, there's a study in the US that defines this disconnect: When asked how they believe they rate with their clients, 85% of BigLaw partners grade themselves an "A+" – they are indispensable! When clients of those same BigLaw lawyers are asked if they would recommend/refer their outside counsel to another in-house colleague, only 35% say 'yes'.

So if that's the year-over-year spread on client dissatisfaction and a clear demonstration of the lack of alignment between clients and BigLaw (whom they view as – at best – fungible), why hasn't 65% of BigLaw been fired or replaced? Answer: Because everyone keeps forgetting who in-house counsel – even the best and brightest – are the vast majority are former lawyers in big law firms, where they were trained and rewarded in the same dysfunctional service model that their outside counsel continue to practice in. Just because they're aware that the Emperor isn't really wearing any clothes now that they're in-house, doesn't mean that they're equipped to know what to do about it. And they're inherently suspicious of New Law environments, just like their BigLaw colleagues: they never left law firms to join Riverview Law or Valorem or Axiom ... they left law firms to land in corporations that often house teams of lawyers who behave more like in-house law firms than innovative service providers. It takes time and the proper in-house incubator for a recovering outside counsel to be reborn as a savvy in-house client.

It takes time for them to learn that their clients don't have legal problems, they have business problems.

But here's the good news. I think the time is now. I'm seeing a critical mass of clients who are ready to do something more than talk about these issues. They're ready to ask for more than a discount.

I think we're finally at the point where enough solid providers, and enough solid clients are trying out New Law services with demonstrated success and engaging with each other about them in commonplace conversation, see, e.g., this very blog comment chain!; the tipping point has arrived.

The in-house leaders I work with are ready – they are still working on the "how" and developing confidence in their decisions and the balance they're striking in connecting risk (of change) and reward, but they are clearly ready to engage in a new round of convergence conversations with their firms (and an increasing array of non-law-firm providers) that will redefine the legal marketplace to reward so many of my good friends posting here who've been patient and diligent leaders in moving us toward better practices. Distinguishing value (and the resulting sustainable business with top clients it will earn) requires far more that quality lawyers performing quality services.

Bottom line: Scoring an 8 – or heck, even a 10 – for having great lawyers is about to become the floor for future in-house retention. I know many of the global departments working on massive change, and what many are driving toward in both their insourcing and outsourcing decisions.

Many clients not only employ their own lawyers, but they also rely on secondments when needed. **Peter Carayiannis** explained why this is a service NewLaw firms are well positioned to deliver. Peter Carayiannis (#11)

[...] In terms of demographics, I will leave it to sociologists to explain the mindset of young professionals (Gen Y). The bottom line is that Gen Y mocks the billable hour and will not spend a career toiling on a billable hour basis. These young professionals have been told they are knowledge workers and that they can work wherever and whenever and need not be fixed to a single location. Consequently, they will work on a flexible and distributed basis, and the clients are insisting that this be offered (nothing new here ... this is the secondment model). The critical difference here is that BigLaw loses money on a fixed fee secondment due to the sunk costs associated with the shiny BigLaw offices in the towers. NewLaw will charge less and make money on a secondment because the related expenses are appropriate to the business opportunity. [...]

Outsourcing to a NewLaw provider is a step beyond secondment. **Karl Chapman** pointed out the unusual situation of in-house legal departments being allowed by BigLaw to hire their own lawyers rather than pay BigLaw fees, because to do so costs them less. He asked 'What supply chain would create a situation where it is cheaper for the customers to do it themselves?' Karl Chapman (#41)

Innovative service providers can disrupt the legal market by leveraging the advantages that come from starting with a blank sheet. While an increase in in-house counsel saves in the short-term, professional outsourcers will be more efficient in the long run, as demonstrated by examples in recruitment.

1) It is clearly important to talk about business models. No single business model will win in the new legal market emerging. However, some models will struggle and prove unfit for purpose – like the traditional law firm model. Others, such as professional outsourcing and resourcing models, are fit for purpose and timely for much of the corporate legal market. This is not to say that some law firms won't be winners, big winners, because they will be. But, taking a ten year, view I wouldn't invest in a traditional law firm; the competition (which is well capitalised and run like businesses) has only just started to flex its muscles. As Reagan said 'you ain't seen nothing yet'.

2)   The legal market is a multi-billion £ global market. It has been (and still is!) protected by myth and regulation. It has generated excess profits for BigLaw participants and has led to incumbent complacency and a lack of innovation. It is hardly surprising therefore that, as the market opens up, it has it will attract the attention of well capitalised new entrants. These new entrants have all the advantages that come from starting with a blank piece of paper. These entrants will disrupt at many levels – customer service, higher quality, innovative pricing, application of MI and data to avoid 'failure demand, targeting specific sectors/niches … etc. This has huge implications for customers and BigLaw.

3)   We've witnessed a number of big themes since we launched Riverview Law in Feb 2012 but the most significant is the speed with which GCs in large corporations have adopted our Legal Advisory Outsourcing model. We are 3-4 years ahead of where we thought we'd be with large businesses and, as you'd expect from a customer-focused business, we've transferred a lot of our investment into this area. But here's the key … the Legal Advisory Outsourcing model we're deploying now is the same model, with a few tweaks, that we deployed in Recruitment Outsourcing throughout the 1990s. It is the same HR Advisory Model AdviserPlus, a

shareholder in Riverview Law, has deployed since 2000. For customers it is proven, low risk and effective.

4)   One theme that never ceases to shock me – and it says a lot about the market in the UK – is the trend for GCs to grow the size of their inhouse functions. When you ask them why they are doing this their answer is simple – it's cheaper for them to employ lawyers than use law firms. What supply chain would create a situation where it is cheaper for the customers to do it themselves? Interestingly, I think that this is just a short-term, unsustainable, labour arbitrage. With a few exceptions (e.g. Cisco) it will be very hard for a GC to sustain the cost savings and quality. To do so requires a fundamental change in the culture and the way in-house functions work plus significant investment in IT. So, while today GCs may be able to do it cheaper in-house, they will never be able do it cheaper and better in the short and medium term than a professional outsourcer with a business model that has talented people (a mix of lawyers and nonlawyers), supported by great IT and heavy R&D spend, who are underpinned by a one team culture and business insight driven by comprehensive MI and data analysis; and This brings me right back to where I started – business models. It's taken me a while to be able to articulate it, but when I'm asked 'So, why do you think Riverview Law will succeed' my answer is now quite simple – 'we have the DNA of a professional outsourcer not a law

firm.' Over the last 25 years we've built big businesses in the recruitment and HR advisory markets by identifying and exploiting market trends (and we knew little about either market when we started). This is the biggest market opportunity we've seen so far – what a great time to be in the legal market!

So in-house counsel is on the rise, both directly competing with BigLaw and starting to direct demand away from BigLaw towards more efficient NewLaw lower cost choices.

RESPONSES SO FAR

As **Peter Kalis** (#43) and others pointed out in Chapter 3, BigLaw – or at least its firms' leaders – is fully aware of these challenges. Some comments related to BigLaw firms taking steps to adjust their business model. Ken Jagger (#4)

[...] I agree with Joel Barolsky that the strength and resilience of BigLaw should not be underestimated. Their head start is considerable. From my recent discussions with the leaders of some of these firms in Australia, it is clear to me that they understand the issues that you raise in your post and are moving to address them. This was not necessarily the case even 12 months ago. [...] I wonder if some firms are not considering incurring the pain and costs of incorporation? If they are not, they should be.

Liam Brown similarly saw an increasing awareness by BigLaw of 'the need to balance the demands from their clients to reduce costs and the demands from their partnership owners for profits' and highlighted a trickling uptake by BigLaw of NewLaw strategies. Liam Brown (#4.1)

Nimble, investor-backed NewLaw companies have filled the gap in the market left by slow-to-adapt BigLaw. But now they must deliver liquidity and ROI over the next few years, just as BigLaw leaders have gained the support of their partnerships to launch NewLaw business model innovations, ranging from alternative resourcing to efficiency initiatives.

No-one should underestimate the leadership of BigLaw firms. They understand the need to balance the demands from their clients to reduce costs and the demands from their partnership owners for profits. I personally don't see this dynamic as much different from the NewLaw firms owned by institutional investors who typically invest one year and seek to maximize profits and exit just a few years later.

Based on my own experience, I believe that most of BigLaw has a longer term view of the legal sector than most of NewLaw. 10 years ago or so when I started working with BigLaw firms like Clifford Chance, DLA, etc. on their legal efficiency initiatives, it was fair to say that most managing partners hadn't yet identified the structural changes in client buying behaviors that were emerging (though leaders at some firms like Baker & McKenzie and Orrick were far-sighted enough to do so and to do something about it).

While BigLaw firms were initially slow to put together the picture of how their clients were changing the way they managed their legal budgets and spend, that gap was quickly filled by nimble entrepreneurs (like you and me!) at a handful of alternative providers. Most of the investors in those alternative providers have already sold their stakes (or are trying to sell) and overall I see a net exit of outside capital. But BigLaw hasn't been sleeping. I am working with a number of BigLaw firms adapting to the changes in the sector. In some cases they are adopting NewLaw business model initiatives (e.g. alternative resourcing and LPO). In some cases they are simply improving efficiency, (e.g. LPM, process efficiency, automation, outsourcing or relocating support services). Despite the popular commentary to the contrary, they aren't standing still.

Liam also reported some important examples of BigLaw–NewLaw cooperation. Liam Brown (#39)

Well, on 31 October 2013 more of BigLaw kind of started operating according to NewLaw business model principles. LeClairRyan is using UnitedLex's capital and know-how to launch its 400 person Legal Solutions Center. And SeyfarthShaw announced they are using NeotaLogic's expert systems, document automation and process control technology to improve the efficiency of their lawyers. BigLaw is experimenting.

This is by no means a comprehensive analysis of how BigLaw firms are addressing the significant challenges to their once-successful business model. If BigLaw firms are aware of them, then many seem not to regard such challenges as relevant. And where a firm's leadership is willing to address the challenges, they face significant resistance from their partners because of the cultural and profit implications. Even if they can deliver better value propositions to clients, BigLaw firms still face significant competition from in-house law departments and increasingly from NewLaw firms. NewLaw, in comparison, is on the move without the baggage of legacy cultures and systems.

USEFUL SOURCES

Beaton, George, 'Law firms are worrying about the wrong things' on Beaton Capital, Bigger. Better. Both? (19 March 2012)
http://www.beatoncapital.com/2012/03/law-firms-are-worrying-aboutthe-wrong-things/

Beaton, George, 'PPEP levels are doomed without re-invention' on Beaton Capital, Bigger. Better. Both? (5 September 2012)
http://www.beatoncapital.com/2012/09/ppep-levels-are-doomedwithout-re-invention/

Christensen, Clayton M, Wang, Dina and van Beverp, Derek 'Consulting on the cusp of disruption' (2013) 91(10) Harvard Business Review 106
http://hbr.org/2013/10/consulting-on-the-cusp-of-disruption/

Henderson, William D, 'From Big Law to Lean Law' (2013) International Review of Law and Economics, in press
http://www.sciencedirect.com/science/article/pii/S0144818813000458

MacEwen, Bruce, 'Growth is Dead: Part 1 - Setting the Stage' on Adam Smith Esq. Blog (4 September 2012)
http://www.adamsmithesq.com/2012/09/growth-is-dead-part-i/

Ribstein, Larry E, 'The Death of Big Law' [2010] Wisconsin Law Review 749
http://wisconsinlawreview.org/wp-content/files/1-Ribstein.pdf

CHAPTER 5.
NEWLAW'S ALTERNATIVE RULES

Having discussed the strength and resilience of BigLaw and the challenges faced by firms based on its model, it is time to turn to NewLaw. A provocative Twitter conversation provided an example of how NewLaw firms are viewed and how they see themselves. This leads to an introduction to the characteristics of the NewLaw business model and a comparison between the BigLaw and the NewLaw business models. I then propose the first published typology for NewLaw. A post by **Eric Chin** – in which the word 'NewLaw' was coined – suggested the growth of Axiom Law, an archetypal NewLaw firm, is a harbinger of just how much market share NewLaw firms may acquire in the future.

To illustrate NewLaw's value propositions, **Karl Chapman** raised the increased efficiency of an experienced outsourcer, while **Ken Grady** pointed to increased vertical integration. For **Jeremy Szwider**, it was about 'getting it', both the changing circumstances and clients' needs. **Steven Tyndall** seconded that and in addition raised the way that NewLaw uses technology to shape, rather than just support, processes. **Richard Burcher** rounded out the discussion by describing the importance of client-centered, more flexible and innovative pricing strategies in NewLaw – and BigLaw – alike.

CHARACTERISTICS OF NEWLAW

Changes in the legal services market are occurring rapidly in response to changing and unmet demand. NewLaw firms are mushrooming in response to these changes.

The following Twitter exchange provided an illustration of the nature of NewLaw firms as they enter the arena. These four Tweets were posted on Twitter during my address to the Law Firm Strategic Leaders Forum in London in October 2012.

Carl White
@cxinlaw

"@grbeaton_law refers to 'barbarians at the gate' who don't belong to traditional law firm club inc @RiverviewLaw + Coop Legal + Keystone Law #SLF2012"

10.38am Oct 24, 2012

Charles Christian
@ChristianUncut

"@grbeaton_law Just been pondering etymology of 'barbarians' bit.ly/TTGRcL Yes an average day in the office with Karl"

10.41am Oct 24, 2012

Mitch Kowalski
@MEKowalski

"Yes, @KarlChapman100 will be the one in animal skins | 'barbarians at the gate' earlier ref @ChristianUncut @grbeaton_law"

10.42am Oct 24, 2012

Riverview Law
@RiverviewLaw

"@grbeaton_law Not at gate! When we got there gate was left open by supply chain that lost touch with its customers"

10.45am Oct 24, 2012

There is already a large and growing variety of NewLaw firms. Based on these types of NewLaw, Beaton Capital has identified the hallmarks of the NewLaw business model based on the firms in our sample that are shown in the table of NewLaw firms in the Appendix. The hallmarks of NewLaw have been grouped in the same way as those of BigLaw in Chapter 3: Human capital, technology, practice economics, ownership structure and fees. They are shown in the table below.

Categories	Hallmarks of NewLaw		Consequences
Human capital	Deployment of talent with the requisite legal and process skills		Efficient division of labour
	Practitioners striving to deliver service to fit-for-purpose standards		Culture of efficiency and effectiveness
	Selling and producing work are separated		Efficient and effectives use of skills
	Promotion of corporate brands		Reduced key person dependency and greater brand strength
Technology	Use of disruptive technologies		'More for less' client benefits
Practice economics	Flexi-work practices that match supply to demand		Low fixed costs
	No tournament		Fewer inappropriate signals
Ownership structure	Corporate ownership		Shareholder value mindset
	Non-lawyer shareholders		Access to capital and alignment of all employees' interests
Fees	Fixed fees		Risk is shared

The NewLaw and BigLaw models share the use of qualified and licensed legal talent. This leads one to conclude a priori that they also share a common commitment to client-centric, ethical behaviour. The ethical challenges present in both business models are discussed in more detail by Professor Moorhead in chapter 7.

It is evident that the BigLaw and NewLaw business models are different in almost every other respect. NewLaw firms are completely re-engineering their underlying business model for delivering legal services. The differences between these NewLaw hallmarks and those of BigLaw are discussed in more detail in the post 'How to recognise a NewLaw firm' on the Beaton Capital blog, Bigger. Better. Both? which is set out below.

So far we have examined the nature of NewLaw firms and glimpsed their potential to change the legal services market. Now let us turn to a more detailed analysis of what the range of NewLaw firms looks like.

NEWLAW TYPOLOGY

How to recognise a NewLaw firm

To varying degrees, NewLaw firms share certain broad characteristics that can be used to group them. And to contrast them with BigLaw firms.

In today's rapidly changing legal landscape it is important to define and be able to recognise NewLaw firms and the many variations. Mark Harris, CEO and Co-founder of Axiom Law, said in a July 19, 2013 interview on Bloomberg Law 'It's a challenge to describe us when we're creating a new category'. The 'new category' to which Mark Harris refers is NewLaw, the name given to it by Eric Chin of Beaton Capital. A closer look at the types of NewLaw firm Beaton Capital has analysed suggests that NewLaw business models are a heterogeneous category.

Since the first NewLaw firms emerged in the late 1960s, entrepreneurial lawyers, business people, and clients of law firms have been investing in new ways of delivering legal services and processes. The result is the emergence of a broad category of NewLaw entities with many variations or types within. The following table proposes a way of understanding the different types of NewLaw that are emerging.

A typology of NewLaw

Types of NewLaw and examples		Human capital	Disruptive technology	Practice economics	Corporate ownership	Fixed fees
NewLaw service providers	A	✓	✓	✓	✓	✓
Virtual legal service providers	B	✓	✓	✓	✓	✓
LPOs	C	✓		✓	✓	✓
Online legal marketplaces	D	✓	✓		✓	✓
Client captives	E	✓		✓	✓	✓
Legal document suppliers	F	✓	✓		✓	✓
Fixed fee traditional law firms	G					✓

The following examples are illustrative, although not all will necessarily agree the choices fit perfectly into their types:

A) Axiom Law, AdventBalance, Riverview Law, Slater & Gordon Ltd
B) Clearspire, Virtual Law
C) Pangea3, Exigent LPO
D) LawyerSelect, LegalMatch
E) In-house law departments, including new forms such as BT Law Ltd and Carillion Legal
F) Epoq, LegalZoom, LawDepot
G) Valorem Law, Marque Lawyers

Hybrids are found in those firms that show characteristics of more than one type. Legal Force (formerly Trademarkia), Rocket Lawyer and LawPath for example do not fit neatly in just one type and are in fact 'Virtual legal service providers' which are also 'Legal document suppliers'.

I conclude that a continuum exists. It ranges from near pure forms of NewLaw, such as Axiom Law, through the seven types to BigLaw. Whether fixed fee BigLaw firms are one or the other is moot. In the main, firms like Valorem Law and Marque Lawyers are much more like BigLaw than NewLaw, but it appears that their mindsets are moving in the NewLaw direction.

It is clear NewLaw firms cannot meet all forms of clients' needs. Nor for that matter can BigLaw firms meet all clients' needs cost-effectively. For example, large, complex and fast moving matters such as those found in takeovers and disputes are and will remain the domain of BigLaw. In consumer markets, as the UK is demonstrating, NewLaw firms are rapidly becoming the providers of choice for legal services.

In 2010 the late Professor Larry E Ribstein of the University of Illinois College of Law wrote The Death of Big Law. He comprehensively argued BigLaw firms (which he labeled Big Law to connote business model and size) are in dire trouble. The rapid success of NewLaw firms described here confirms this.

I have no doubt about the continuing importance of BigLaw firms in our economies, but the time is now for re-thinking and re-inventing.

George Beaton
@grbeaton_law

"Response to my tweet inviting suggestions for a collective noun for Axiom et al: 'Succession' 'Alternative' 'Challenge 'Clarion'"

7.47am Jul 26, 2012

In addition, this relevant Tweet question highlighted the advantages of corporate ownership that NewLaw appears to enjoy:

Stephen Mayson
@StephenMayson

"@cxinlaw @bhamiltonbruce MT @grbeaton_law: Why is 'non-lawyer' ownership such a terrible thing? @StephenMayson wp.me/p1rQgF-6y Thx all"

9.32pm May 10, 2012

NewLaw firms share certain characteristics and these can be contrasted with those of BigLaw. Across the spectrum of NewLaw firms there are opportunities to offer more and possibly better choices for clients. And rewards for NewLaw firms themselves.

THE POTENTIAL OF NEWLAW

There is to my knowledge no data on the market share of all NewLaw firms defined in this manner. But given the total combined revenues of all law firms lie somewhere around USD500billion globally, one can safely say the current market share is well below one percent. There is, however, already significant growth in some NewLaw firms – and much of it is at the expense of BigLaw firms. A case in point is the growth of Axiom Law since its first income in 2002. Using historical data to calculate Axiom and DLA Piper's (currently BigLaw's largest firm) compound annual growth rates, **Eric Chin** at Beaton Capital predicts that Axiom could outgrow DLA Piper by 2018. Eric Chin: '2018 – The year Axiom becomes the world's largest legal services firm'

The 'NewLaw' neologism is introduced as the antithesis of BigLaw. A future where Axiom, a NewLaw firm, could become the world's largest legal services provider by 2018 is contemplated.

The stratospheric rise of substitutes (in the Michael Porter sense) for traditional BigLaw firms is witnessing the emergence and growth of firms like Axiom Law, Riverview Law, Keystone Law, and AdventBalance, to name just a few.

To describe these substitutes I have coined the term 'NewLaw'. These firms are designed around virtual workspaces and rely on the rise of supertemps.

Supertemps in this case are lawyers who have been trained by traditional BigLaw firms but are now looking for flexible work arrangements.

These alternative business model (ABM) legal services providers can provide the same or similar service levels to BigLaw for certain types of work – but at or below incumbents' break-even points.

Axiom Law, founded in 2000, is the face of this new group of ABM legal service providers. It has grown its revenue exponentially at 72% compound annual growth rate (CAGR) from 2002 to 2011. During the same period the largest law firm today, DLA Piper, has grown its revenue at 13% CAGR, partly by adding new firms to its network.

Axiom outgrows DLA Piper by 2018

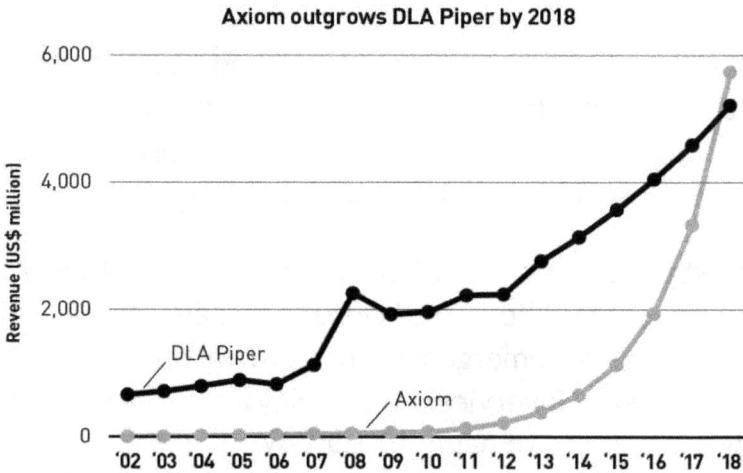

At Axiom's current pace, the firm will outgrow DLA Piper by 2018. That is in five years! Our modeling shows:

1) Axiom, $130m in 2011 and growing at 72% CAGR will have a turnover of $5,730m in 2018
2) DLA Piper, $2,231m in 2011 and growing 13% CAGR will achieve a turnover of $5,215m in 2018, and
3) Axiom would be at least $500m larger than DLA Piper by that time.

These are estimates based on historical data and should be treated with proper caution. But for the sake of this argument, the uptake of clients as evidenced by the growth of at least some NewLaw firms and the plateauing of BigLaw firm's revenues points to a possible future where NewLaw rivals BigLaw for overall market dominance.

As corporate clients continue to exert downward pressure on external legal spending (by reducing price and volume), the more cost-effective ABMs will grow in influence – and size. And one can only guess their profits. And of course in NewLaw profits are not measured by profit-per-partner units. As Clayton Christensen has observed in 'Consulting on the cusp of disruption', as the upstarts [NewLaw] move upmarket, incumbents [BigLaw] are in a danger of losing their clients.

NEWLAW VALUE PROPOSITIONS FOR BUSINESS AND CONSUMER CLIENTS

Karl Chapman (#41) whose comment is set out in full in Chapter 4 is convinced of the client benefits offered by new business models: [...] It is clearly important to talk about business models. No single business model will win in the new legal market emerging. However, some models will struggle and prove unfit for purpose – like the traditional law firm model. Others, such as professional outsourcing and resourcing models, are fit for purpose and timely for much of the corporate legal market. This is not to say that some law firms won't be winners, big winners, because they will be. But, taking a ten-year view I wouldn't invest in a traditional law firm; the competition (which is well capitalised and run like businesses) has only just started to flex its muscles. As Reagan said 'you ain't seen nothing yet'. [...]

Other industries have shifted to project-based, rather than entity-based, ways of managing complex projects. In principle, there seem to be many similarities between producing a big movie and, for example, managing a large takeover. George Beaton (#7.1)

[...] It is instructive to have a close look at what's happening in the so-called 'Hollywood' economy. Decades ago studio moguls owned everything, and everybody required to make a big movie (as large BigLaw firms now do to provide big deal and litigation services). Today the studios are financiers and project managers; all the players are self-employed and contracted by the project (i.e. making the movie). NewLaw financiers and project managers are already emerging. [...]

There is also substantial potential for value adding through legal processes supported by technology that are integrated in innovative ways with client businesses, as **Ken Grady** (#35 set out in full in chapter 7) explained. **Jeremy Szwider** (#40) reported how the border between NewLaw firms and clients is being blurred. NewLaw's willingness to use technology for service delivery, rather than to support established processes, is mentioned by **Steven Tyndall** (#51) below. This might be beneficial in helping clients by 'teaching them how to fish' rather than delivering the fish fingers as BigLaw currently does. Ken Grady (#35)

[...] Clients will vertically integrate legal services (labor and technology) as they continue to recognize the benefits of controlling and inventing their futures (lawyers helping mold the future of businesses through embedding strategic legal solutions into new business development).[...]

Jeremy Szwider similarly argued for closer integration of legal services delivery with client businesses, aided by technological innovation. Jeremy Szwider (#40)

NewLaw is about a revolution in the legal marketplace. Alternative business models (such as LPOs, online legal marketplaces, virtual law firms, commoditisation, etc.) are evidence of this. In some NewLaw firms, the distinction between private practice and in-house is increasingly blurred – incorporating the best aspects of both worlds.

NewLaw is more than just a passing trend. There has most certainly been a shift in the pillars of the legal profession and BigLaw is being challenged. With the economic downturn and the progress of technology, we are witnessing a revolution in the legal marketplace. Alternative business models (such as LPOs, online legal marketplaces, virtual law firms, dispersed law firms, commoditisation etc.) are evidence of this evolution and the creation of NewLaw business models – which are changing the way clients use lawyers and pay for legal services. Our NewLaw business model at Bespoke Law is all about the client, focusing on efficiency, technology, innovation and price certainty – that is the HOW. And for us, importantly, the distinction between private practice and in-house is increasingly blurred – incorporating the best aspects of both worlds.

I draw close analogies to the trends of music consumerism. In the music revolution, technology has helped bring the listener closer to the music. The music revolution has progressed from records, to cassettes, to CDs and then the MP3. The rise of the MP3 has made music much easier to obtain. We now devour as much music as we possibly can, and musicians need to stay on top of their game to maintain their status on an iPod's growing playlist. These trends were clearly not part of our predecessor's wildest dreams as they spun their LP vinyls back in the 50's. But the evolution rolled along, slowly but surely, and the consumer is now much better off for it.

Steve Jobs once said "Innovation has nothing to do with how many R&D dollars you have. When Apple came up with the Mac, IBM was spending at least 100 times more on R&D. It's not about money. It's about the people you have, how you're led, and how much you get it." The legal profession does not have the privilege of having a leader like Steve Jobs at its fingertips. However, there appears to be enough innovators and disruptors looking from the outside in and helping us push the boundaries to evolve the legal profession. Some may simply call it an iteration or an evolution in the legal marketplace ... or maybe even a revolution.

Overall, there is little doubt that both BigLaw and NewLaw intend to use technology to provide legal services in an efficient manner to satisfy clients' needs. But how much technology improves the end-product or enables a similar or better product to be delivered for less fundamentally depends on the view of the role of technology in the process of producing legal advice. Once again, this is about sustaining versus disruptive innovation, as **Steven Tyndall** summed up. Steven Tyndall (#51)

BigLaw typically asks 'How can I use technology to do what I do better?' Whereas NewLaw simply asks 'How can it be done better?'. The first question results in sustaining technology. The second question does not just reference technology; it is an intrinsic component. NewLaw will therefore better use technology.

As a legal IT professional I just had to chime in with my two Bitcoins to support fully the comment "Innovation has nothing to do with how many R&D dollars you have".

As cloud computing reaches maturity, even the smallest firms and inhouse teams will be able to subscribe to powerful systems with intelligent analytics; systems they were previously unable to afford or support internally.

Better use of technology is intrinsically linked to which question is asked. BigLaw typically asks 'How can I use technology to do what I do better?' Whereas NewLaw simply asks 'How can it be done better?'

The first question may seem like a good one to ask but will almost certainly (likely) result in implementing some form of sustaining technology. In turn, this technology will then have most of its powerful capabilities reduced in trying to make it support 'what I do'.

The second question–correctly in my view–does not specifically refer to technology per se, because it is not an afterthought. Nor indeed, is it the point. A successful online store is not successful simply because it is online.

I see that firms operating with 'NewLaw' thinking will make better use of technology. By seeing results they will be more likely to invest further in technology and will move from strength to strength.

So NewLaw competes on price and product, often by offering commoditised services for a good deal less, or offering services that add value by being more closely integrated with the client's business through people and technology. Another aspect of a more flexible business revolves around pricing. Innovative pricing is of course open equally to BigLaw and NewLaw firms, as **Richard Burcher** explained when he drew attention to the importance of choosing and negotiating pricing strategies that accommodate clients' needs as well as firms' profit motives. Richard Burcher (#48)

New Law firms are characterised by amongst other things, high levels of sophistication around pricing governance. Analytics and execution not only yield higher profit margins. Equally importantly they engender client loyalty and endorsement through a tangible demonstration of 'cost consciousness' and alignment of the firms' financial interests with those of clients.

I would like to offer a small contribution from the perspective of pricing, something that will be fundamental to the NewLaw model. Clients now expect their lawyers to provide greater:

1) cost consciousness
2) pricing and payment options
3) client involvement and engagement in pricing
4) pricing transparency
5) pricing certainty and budgetary predictability – a 'no-surprises' policy
6) 6) correlation between price and perceived value of the outcome and
7) price risk sharing.

These will need to be the hallmarks of NewLaw's approach to pricing but for now, most firms are relatively poorly equipped to deliver these requirements.

There is no right or wrong method of pricing. It is only right or wrong for a certain client on a particular matter. Pricing alchemy occurs when the most judicious blend of pricing and payment options are conceived and deployed on a case-by-case basis.

Firms need to understand that all pricing tactics available to lawyers (and they need to master at least a dozen to be effective) sit on a price risk continuum; a concept that remains poorly understood other than as a by-product of partners' instinctive reluctance to give clients firm quotes.

The up-front agreed allocation of price risk between the firm and the client presents challenges and opportunities. Poorly executed, it will produce lost margin or even large write-offs. Assessed and deployed effectively, it can have a swift and profoundly positive effect on margins and pricing palatability from the clients' perspective.

Moreover, we do not need to confine ourselves to offering clients pricing choice. We also can offer payment choice, a strategy that is largely ignored or dismissed. The default setting is that the client must comply with the firms' standard terms and conditions around payment. But that inflexibility not only irritates clients, it also obscures opportunities to secure work we might otherwise miss out on or work that we might secure a premium on if only we were little more accommodating.

In summary, providing the client with well-conceived and articulated pricing and payment choices greatly increases the prospect of striking a deal that works well for the client and the firm.

Alex Hamilton (comment #16.2 in the original thread) agreed with the importance risk-assumed fixed pricing by the legal services provider and stressed that it provides a strong incentive to manage matters efficiently by deploying resources over the life cycle of a project. He also raised the possibility of using on-demand software development based on open-source material to originate support tools on a flexible, trial-and-error basis, echoing a view of technology as informing, rather than supporting, best practice processes.

In summary, NewLaw firms are characterised by innovative business strategies. These include process optimisation with the outcomes-directed mind-set of an outsourcer, closer technological integration with the client business, and pricing strategies that can be contrasted with the prevailing norms of the BigLaw model. These and other strategies provide clients with real alternatives to BigLaw rules.

USEFUL SOURCES

Beaton, George, 'Last days of the BigLaw business model' on Beaton Capital, Bigger. Better. Both? (6 September 2013)
http://www.beatoncapital.com/2013/09/last-days-biglaw-business-model/

Beaton, George, 'How to recognise a NewLaw firm' on Beaton Capital, Bigger. Better. Both? (11 December) <
http://www.beatoncapital.com/2013/12/recognise-newlaw-firm/>

Christensen, Clayton 'Disruptive Innovation' (7 December 2014)
http://www.claytonchristensen.com/key-concepts/

Christensen, Clayton M, Wang, Dina and van Bever, Derek 'Consulting on the cusp of disruption' (2013) 91 (10) Harvard Business Review 106 http://hbr.org/2013/10/consulting-on-the-cusp-of-disruption/

Chin, Eric, '2018 - The year Axiom becomes the world's largest legal services firm' on Beaton Capital, Bigger. Better. Both? (13 September 2013) <http://www.beatoncapital.com/2013/09/2018-year-axiom-becomes-worlds-largestlegal-services-firm/>

Ribstein, Larry E, 'The Death of Big Law' [2010] Wisconsin Law Review 749 http://wisconsinlawreview.org/wp-content/files/1-Ribstein.pdf

CHAPTER 6.
TESTING NEW LAW

Despite some hubris, nobody believes NewLaw will overtake BigLaw in the legal services marketplace. The strength and resilience of BigLaw as an industry discussed in Chapter 3 is, however, being tested and questioned. **Ross Dawson** highlighted the sheer force of the status quo in a conservative, risk-averse sector made up of traditional firms and clients. NewLaw will have to compete strongly for its share of the market. In addition, future recruitment of suitably trained lawyers looms as a problem for NewLaw. **Nicole Bradick** drew attention to the lack of sufficient early legal career training in NewLaw firms. **Jordan Furlong** affirmed the declining number of training opportunities in BigLaw, which trains both lawyers who stay on and those who 'defect' to set up or join NewLaw firms.

While there is some training in NewLaw, as **Patrick Lamb** indicated, this does not seem to extend to early career training. **Silvia Hodges Silverstein** raised several questions about both legal education and early career training in general as necessary against the backdrop of the drastic changes in the legal industry. Some potential answers may be found in the recent New York City Bar report Developing legal careers and developing justice in the 21st century; this was summarised by **Imme Kaschner**.

CHALLENGES

The earliest forms of NewLaw firm started in 1969 with CPA Global (Computer Patent Annuities) in the Channel Islands by UK patent attorneys to handle patent renewals. Others emerged in the 1990s when Epoq started using document automation technology and online delivery to tailor legal documents to an individual client's circumstances.

NewLaw chronology

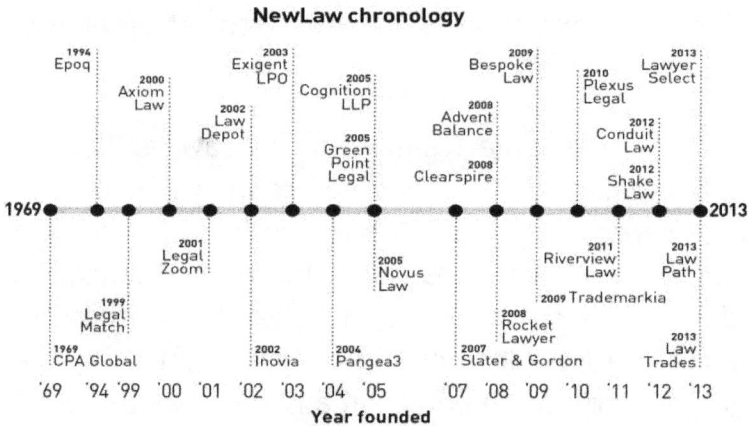

Year founded

This timeline illustrates the emergence of a range of NewLaw firms. The many types of NewLaw described in Chapter 5 are represented in this chart. They range from Exigent – a LPO – to Slater & Gordon – the world's first listed law firm – to Axiom Law – the NewLaw crown prince. These firms extend from stock exchange giants to small start-ups.

With the innovators in the provision of legal services out in uncharted waters, there will no doubt be successes and failures among individual firms. What will make one firm succeed and another fail was not explicitly examined in the thread. But a few related themes emerged which deserve to be mentioned.

Regardless of how differentiating their service delivery value propositions may be, NewLaw firms still must build trust with clients. None have trusted brands even faintly approaching those of well-established BigLaw firms.

The 'comfort and ease of integrated relationships' between clients and BigLaw, as **Ross Dawson** termed it, form very powerful organisational bonds. Ross Dawson (#17)

Distributed legal services models have big potential to serve clients. Clients will choose between the efficiency offered by these newer models and the comfort and convenience offered by traditional law firms.

There is massive potential from distributed professional services models, yet there are significant constraints as well.

The foundations have now been laid for a significant acceleration of new legal services models. However, while the impact could be severe on some legal firms and sectors, the erosion *may* be muted for the more resilient firms.

Ultimately, ease of use and comfort are unlikely to retard the uptake of lower-cost substitutes for established services. In a recent HBR blog post 'Why Law Firm Pedigree May Be a Thing of the Past' Wang and Dattu presented data showing that of the general counsel in major corporations 74 % were more likely to use a less well-known firm (provided both offered 'good lawyers') for a difference of 30% in the price.

This requirement for 'good lawyers' raises problems, particularly the way NewLaw currently recruits legal talent laterally, as opposed to investing in training as BigLaw does. This could limit the sustainability of NewLaw firms. **Nicole Bradick** summed this up. Nicole Bradick (#33)

There is concern over the future of training for lawyers if BigLaw continues to contract. NewLaw firms currently rely on BigLaw to train young lawyers and bless them with pedigree. The hope is that NewLaw of the future will train lawyers; when this occurs BigLaw may lose some of its attraction.

So much of NewLaw (including companies I have started and/or am involved with) announce that they offer top-tier legal talent at lower cost due to a lean and agile infrastructure. NewLaw clients love that they are getting a former BigLaw partner for a great rate due to the reduction in overhead and the lack of partner leverage. A lawyer with BigLaw experience is still very much a draw for clients of NewLaw firms. Perhaps over time this focus on pedigree will erode as new models take hold, but for now it seems that NewLaw needs BigLaw to train lawyers and needs BigLaw to be an undesirable place so that great talent leaves BigLaw to go to a new model firm!

I have not yet heard of a new model firm that takes new grads and provides them with any real substantive training. That's because these new firms, with a focus on reducing overhead, cannot justify billing a client for attorney training time. I think for the foreseeable future we'll need firms with big overhead and clients willing to pay for it to train the next generation of NewLaw lawyers... although I do think there is a considerable opportunity out there for a new model that offers to supervise and train new lawyers in a way that is profitable and beneficial to clients.

So in addition to all the obstacles usually facing new market entrants competing with well-resourced and established incumbents, NewLaw (in conjunction with the organised legal profession and legal educators) will have to address the shortage of training that will only increase as NewLaw grows.

CONSEQUENCES AND RESPONSES

Jordan Furlong saw a need for legal educators and the legal profession to start addressing the changes in the delivery of legal services by instituting changes in legal graduate- and post-graduate education. Jordan Furlong (#33.3)

Large firms have now made it clear that they're no longer going to employ many new lawyers, and whether that is good or bad is secondary to the fact that it's happening and it's unlikely to change anytime soon.

We should be careful not to conflate "experience in a large law firm" with "new lawyer training" — they are not necessarily the same thing at all. Three years in a large law firm will teach you how to be a profitable generator of revenue for that firm. But it will not teach you anything about client relations (as you won't meet many clients), business generation (since you'll be fed work created by other people's business generation), or running a successful business (since you're an employee, not an entrepreneur). You may well be enrolled in internal professional development training courses, and some of these are quite good; but there's no guarantee of either outcome. For the most part, employment in a large law firm prepares you for employment in another large law firm.

"New lawyer training" is what the legal profession as a whole needs, and a dire need it is, too. Most law schools don't and won't teach it, and it will be several years before market pressures overcome their structural and cultural impediments to allow them to do so. Most bars admit new lawyers to practice on the basis of a law degree, a test, and an absence of felony convictions, but do not otherwise assess new lawyers for the ability to offer legal services to the public in a competent manner. As I've written elsewhere (e.g. 'CPD and the presumption of confidence and ' The MCLE question no one wants to ask '), we don't really have a professional process or infrastructure in place that can defensibly ensure the competence of new private law practitioners.

We, as a profession, have for many years been relying on large law firms to employ great numbers of new lawyers, and we've been closing our eyes and wishing very hard that this employment amounts to "new lawyer training." It doesn't. Large firms have now made clear they're no longer going to employ many new lawyers, and whether that's good or bad is secondary to the fact that it's happening and it's unlikely to change anytime soon. So now we must face our longstanding failure to create and enforce a discipline of new lawyer training and move to address it as soon as possible. I suggest that we get on that.

Now and for the foreseeable future I believe NewLaw will enjoy a dependent relationship with BigLaw. The latter firms – and their clients – are doing the heavy lifting, training lawyers who later join NewLaw. It's hard to see how this will play out. There was, and to a large degree still is I suspect, a professional ethos in BigLaw that says: It's part of our contribution to the profession and society to train young lawyers. If this willingness and capacity to invest dwindles, all stakeholders will be the poorer unless NewLaw or others find ways to do the same. This is regardless of the exact quality of training at BigLaw.

Patrick Lamb (#33.1) asserted a deterioration in BigLaw training now compared with 'decades past' and stated that for NewLaw 'being better faster helps improve our margins', and investment in training is therefore part of the business model. That said, this probably more about on-the-job-training for experienced lawyers to use new processes than about initial training for new graduates. Patrick Lamb (#33.1)

There is a huge difference in the quality and quantity of training large law firms offered in decades past and what they offer now. It seems likely that the "pedigree" of those paroled from BigLaw will be as important going forward. Firms like ours that do a great deal (or all) of our work on fixed fees place a premium on training since being better, faster helps improve our margins. There is nothing like a direct financial interest–seeing dollars drop to the distributable bottom line–to motivate training.

So much for the need, and probably diminishing opportunities, for law graduate training. Looking at the seismic shift that seems to be happening in the delivery of legal services, it could be argued this also necessitates a shift in the way that lawyers are educated and trained at university and on entry to practice. **Silvia Hodges Silverstein** raised several important questions. Silvia Hodges Silverstein (#50)

The key questions for the New Legal Curriculum are:

1) How do we educate future generations of lawyers so they are prepared to succeed in 2020 and beyond? and
2) What will the role of the lawyer be in 2020?

Thinking like a lawyer needs to be thinking like a value-creating legal issues problem-solver.

This summer, Strategies magazine, the Legal Marketing Association's trade publication, asked me for my vision of the law firm in 2020. Here's what I came up with.

'You step out of the shower after your morning jog on the beach. You are the chief client officer at Legal Inc. International, the world's largest provider of legal services. "Congratulations, your company stocks just went up 10%, you should treat yourself with a nice weekend get-away" you hear your virtual assistant saying via the sound-system.

Smiling, you get dressed and head over to the virtual meeting area in your home office to join your colleagues Ivan, Paramjit, Rafiq and Wei-Ting. Funny, you work with them all the time but have only met Paramjit in person at an industry event a few months ago. You're still getting used to seeing them as holograms rather than on the work surface that is as large as your desk. Wei-Ting, your newest team member is beaming: "I just ran the analysis: According to our pitch probability prediction model, we have a 78% chance of winning the pitch that came in last night." "What's their lifetime customer value to us?" you ask. Ivan vigorously types on his screen. It takes less than 2 seconds before the number – $750m – pops up on your screen. "And they always pay fast" adds Rafiq. "Well, you know what to do, I'd run process 101 and assemble the team" you say, smiling at her. "Let's make it 100%!".

So, while I might not see my colleagues as holograms then, I would bet on a future of data-driven, professionally run law corporations in 2020. That's what NewLaw looks like in my book; the natural development of a more traditional, often inefficient and sometimes semi-artisanal way of working. The question I'm asking myself when I teach my students in law firm management and marketing at Columbia Law School and Fordham Law School is how do we need to educate the next generation of lawyers so they are prepared to succeed in 2020? What tools do we need to give them?

Nobody argues that a lawyer needs to have sound legal training. But I am not sure the argument that we need to train them to "think like lawyers" convinces me. If "thinking like a lawyer training" means that we let them graduate with a mere legal lens of the world, we probable don't want them to think like (traditional) lawyers. This is no longer enough. Why would it make sense to train people in the old way for a new environment? But perhaps the bigger issue here is to first define what should be the role of a lawyer in 2020 before even discussing new business models. Whatever this NewLaw business model will be, it needs to serve the clients. Better, some would argue, more efficiently, others would say. Clients need solutions for business problems that have a legal angle. That is what the next generation needs to embrace. Rather than thinking like 'legal issues interpreters' or 'habitual objection raisers' – as a GC recently referred to traditional lawyers – or as 'legal theorists', lawyers need to think like 'value-creating legal issues problem-solvers'.

So let's brainstorm. What should the training look like for someone who is a 'value-creating legal issues problem-solver'? As corporate risk managers, should we put more focus on this aspect, coupled with a view to come up with efficient and business-minded solutions? Rather than litigating or resolving disputes out of court, should their training focus more on the prevention of legal issues? Or do they all need basic general business and management training? Can and should we expect them to be able to read and interpret balance sheets and income statements? In fact, should they understand where profits come from, what the typical cost drivers are? Some technology training perhaps? And what should we do so they are able to decide what work humans should do and what is better left to technology and software solutions? Let's discuss the New Legal Curriculum that incorporates these aspects in 2020, or before.

The choice is (partially) ours. Do we want a world that looks backwards or forwards?

These questions are relevant for law graduate and early career training. In thinking about what the appropriate changes might look like and what opportunities there are for innovative post-graduate training, a recent report by the New York City Bar represents a milestone in comprehensive analysis and presentation of ways forward. **Imme Kaschner** summarised some relevant points. Imme Kaschner (#33.5)

Secular trends in the legal services industry necessitate changes in legal education both prior to and after graduation. The recent New York City Bar report Developing legal careers and developing justice in the 21st century shows there are feasible options to do this. Early in-house training and setting up new structures to address unmet civil legal needs with appropriate supervision, open up new ways of early-career legal training.

There is a growing awareness in the legal profession, certainly in the US, that the legal services industry is changing rapidly, and that this has implications for legal education. The New York City Bar report Developing legal careers and developing justice in the 21st century is a recent cogent analysis and prognosis for legal education and early career training. While some of the content and proposed solutions are not necessarily applicable beyond the US, the overview of trends in the legal profession provides valuable insights that seem generally applicable for at least common law jurisdictions.

The report proceeds from an assessment of the situation of recent legal graduates that can only be described as dire. Only 56% of 2011 and 2012 graduates are in full-time positions that require passing legal bar examinations nine months after graduation (pg 17). These graduates have on average tuition debts between $75k (public law schools) and $125k (private law schools) (pg 19).

One reason for the decline in law firm associate positions is the unbundling of the work that clients send to outside law firms. That is, clients are separating matters into discrete tasks and giving each of these tasks to the most efficient provider, in many instances offshore legal process outsourcers. This was work traditionally done by junior associates and provided them with on-the-job training. 'As a result, the opportunities for formative experiences for junior lawyers at many firms are decreasing' (pg 35). While the percentage of graduates entering small practices or forming solo practices is on the rise (pg 38), this poses unique challenges because the traditional law school curriculum does not prepare students to run what is effectively a small business.

At the same time, some in-house legal departments are directly hiring trainees as more efficient way of obtaining legal services, rather than instructing outside law firms (pg 25). These positions are partially compensating for the training lost in law firms.

The report also questions traditional law school casebook teaching methods, suggesting they are ineffective in preparing future lawyers (pg 40). It points to how business schools have modified the casebook method to teach practical decision-making under conditions of uncertainty (pg 45).

As an aside, the contrast between law (research and consider every possible aspect) and business (risk-adjusted assessment of options) school teaching suggests the latter might be better suited to providing commercial legal advice in a fixed cost agreement setting.

The report points to the importance of learning complex problem-solving in teams and experientially through clinics and bridge-to-practice programs (pg 49) to prepare lawyers for a different future.

'Tomorrow's lawyers need more practical experience, skill development and problem-solving practice, in addition to analytical skills honed by more traditional ways of instruction' (pg 8). Experience for students and early-career lawyers in private sector and government legal services are also recommended (pg 54). To allow law schools to do these things, regulations need to change as necessary to allow curriculum innovation.

The report serves as a timely reminder of the need to reform legal education and training to prepare lawyers for the changing landscape.

So overall, innovative NewLaw firms face many challenges when entering the legal services market – and not all of them will succeed. But even for those who do succeed, recruiting legal talent will eventually become a problem if BigLaw continues to lose market share and commensurately reduce trainee numbers.

USEFUL SOURCES

Furlong, Jordan, 'CPD and the Presumption of Confidence' on Slaw-Canada's online legal magazine (30 December 2011)
http://www.slaw.ca/2011/12/30/cpd-and-the-presumption-ofcompetence/

Furlong, Jordan, 'The MCLE question no one wants to ask' on Law21 Blog (1 April 2013) http://www.law21.ca/2013/04/the-mcle-question-no-onewants-to-ask/

New York City Bar, Developing legal careers and developing justice in the 21st century (Fall 2013) http://www2.nycbar.org/pdf/developing-legalcareers-and-delivering-justice-in-the-21st-century.pdf

Wang, Dina and Dattu, Firoz, 'Why Law Firm Pedigree May Be a Thing of the Past' on Harvard Business Review, Harvard Business Review Blog (11 October 2013) http://blogs.hbr.org/2013/10/why-law-firm-pedigree-may-be-athing-of-the-past/

CHAPTER 7.
NEW RULES? AN OUTLOOK

The small representation of BigLaw's voice in this thread is not necessarily evidence of a lack of awareness or preparedness to deal with the challenges BigLaw faces, notwithstanding some facetious Tweets to the contrary. The debate must, however, go beyond a mere comparison of business models as **Paul Lippe** pointed out with reference to the privileged position of the lawyer in society. **Ken Grady** injected a dose of old-fashioned and timely professionalism when he exhorted lawyers to work on winning back the position of the trusted advisor. **Richard Moorhead** finished off with a thought-provoking essay on the ethical challenges that reside in both the BigLaw and NewLaw business models.

Alex Hamilton
@AlexHamiltonRad

"@ronfriedmann @jordan_law21 @grbeaton_law
I do worry that a few 10s or 100s of us live in a
NewLaw echo chamber"

5.10pm Oct 22, 2013

Ron Friedmann
@ronfriedmann

"@jordan_law21 @grbeaton_law I don't worry re
echo chamber - I'm not in the saviour business
and we know results are everything"

3.35pm Oct 22, 2013

AN OUTLOOK

So far the discussion in this thread book has revolved around business models, market trends, technology and clients' buying behaviour. But ultimately the law plays a significant part in the rules that govern society. The way legal services are provided goes beyond organisational structures that reflect market forces. Lawyers have the duty and privilege of interpreting the rules our society has chosen for itself. To a degree, society functions because lawyers provide an interface between democratically agreed rules and those who want to obey by them. **Paul Lippe** (comment #47 in original thread) quipped 'Lawyers do not suffer from "Excess Humility Disorder." So if we (=the lawyers) want to assert and maintain a leading role, we really do have to be purer than Caesar's wife, and act in the broad interest of society, not in our self-interest.'

Given the significant challenges faced by both BigLaw and NewLaw and their need for profitability, fulfilling this mission might be more easily said than done. **Ken Grady** threw down a gauntlet when he said 'Focusing on service brought us wealth. Focusing on wealth brought us to this point. Perhaps focusing again on service will bring us back'. Ken Grady (#35)

Changes affecting the legal services industry are not unique; most industries have experienced similar disruptions. Rather than obsessing about these changes, BigLaw should use them as the opportunity to reinvent themselves. Now is the time for BigLaw to win back the role of C-suite trusted advisor.

I come at this issue with over 30 years in a mix of boutique and mid-size firms and an AmLaw 50 firm, 20 years in-house, and now several weeks as a consultant embedded in an AmLaw 100 environment.

What interests me most about this topic is the inwardness of the discussion. We talk as if we are in the first major industry to face change and reformation. We are, of course, not the first – not even close. Perhaps more accurately, we are one of the last.

Invoking George Santayana: "Those who do not remember the past are condemned to repeat it." The legal industry is going through a phase with a mid-term outcome not hard to predict at a macro level given the history of change in other industries. I see a consensus around the following predictions.

First, technology will replace many labor-intensive activities. This isn't the first and won't be the last time the legal industry faces technology changes.

Second, firms will continue consolidating. Weaker players, big and small, will lose to stronger players. I watched distributors for one of my clients consolidate from 12,000 to 4,000 in less than five years.

Third, concentration will change industry stratification. There will be fewer large law firms and fewer mid-size firms. Conflicts rules will ensure more of each size survive than the market would otherwise support. There will be many small firms, at least in part because there will be many smaller corporate clients who prefer these firms (which, as they do today, will use technology to be competitive).

Fourth, all firms will change operations. Technology will drive some change. Work force values will force some change (e.g. millennials favor technology over office space, life choices over work choices). What clients want will drive some change (e.g. a work force that flexes in size depending on the organization's needs – where Axiom plays, in part).

Fifth, wealth generation opportunities will change. Microsoft was the wealth generation opportunity for Bill Gates. Today it is BigSoftware, and the multitude of startups are the opportunities for wealth generation.

Sixth, clients will vertically integrate legal services (labor and technology) as they continue recognizing the benefits of controlling and inventing their futures (lawyers helping mold the future of businesses through embedding strategic legal solutions into new business development).

The list goes on, but I'm belaboring the point and to all of you it probably seems obvious. Because it is obvious. By looking to what happened when other industries went through such changes, we see the general patterns of what will emerge. Strong, smart, nimble players will survive; slow, inward-focused and tradition-bound players will struggle and disappear. How many of the companies on the original S&P 500 list still exist (when the S&P hit 50 years, only 86 of the original 500 still existed)?

Let's stop obsessing about change in the legal industry. Rather, let's focus on channeling this change to reform the role of lawyers. At one time, we served as trusted advisors to clients, lending our strategic insights, analytical skills and technical abilities to help clients see around corners and shape the future of businesses and society. No, we weren't saints, and this isn't viewing the past through rose-colored glasses. But today, many view lawyers as tools to accomplish necessary (and not very pleasant) tasks – technocrats bringing little additional value. Harsh, perhaps, but in 2011, lawyers had an approval rating of just 29%.

Why not use this opportunity to focus discussions on how to mold the industry back into a highly respected profession, profitable for participants sure, but also respected for the value added. Those who want to take entrepreneurial risks will have plenty of opportunities for wealth generation. But wealth generation should not be our overriding purpose or the focus of our discussions. Focusing on service brought us wealth. Focusing on wealth brought us to this point. Perhaps focusing again on service will bring us back. Maybe the new hashtag could be #RespectedLaw?

This is a worthy sentiment. It seems fitting to conclude this conversation with Richard Moorhead's thoughtful essay warning us that both the BigLaw and the NewLaw business models pose ethical challenges to the practitioner who has, after all, a fiduciary duty towards his client. Richard Moorhead (#49)

In examining the BigLaw–NewLaw contrast in ethical terms we should view neither business model through rose-tinted spectacles nor be mindful the impact of economic incentives on ethical standards of behaviour.

I have been encouraged to think about the issue of the ethics of innovation. It's a big topic, and I cannot do it justice here. But I can try and post some pointers and thoughts; in the hope they provoke discussion. From various quarter were hear, as cri de coeur, the idea that innovation is either saviour or end of the legal profession. Both views are based on slightly different meanings of professionalism. And my intuition, based on reading hundreds of blogs and hearing dozens of speeches on the subject is that the Innovators tend to mean that innovation is the saviour of law as a business and the Traditionalists that business is the problem, and on that basis innovation should be resisted. In reality though, both positions overlap.

From the ethics and infrastructure perspective there is plenty to worry about in the context of big law. Hourly fees and fee padding is one. The economisation of legal work is another. Lawyers compare themselves, their value, their firm's value against economic metrics. It is what gets them promoted; or allows them to swing more swiftly through flexible lockstep. There is a plausible case for saying this makes them less ethical. There is an interesting body of research suggests that the more one is encouraged to think of one's work within a 'business frame' the more likely one is to be unethical. But it is dangerous for law firms to take such research seriously: money is visible, they are chastised by journalists if they seek to make it less visible, and they must compete in the numbers game to keep recruitment and retention stable.

The third worry is the strength of client alignment this generates. Inhouse lawyers are regularly sneered at by private practice cousins for their willingness to do for their employers what 'independent' outside practitioners would not. But if recent scandals have told us one thing it is that private practice firms have been implicated often enough for me to doubt the strength of the distinction made.

Now we could debate whether this rather critical take on the ethicality of BigLaw is accurate or exaggerated. I do not know, but I offer it as a reminder that we should not compare innovation or alternative business structures against overly rose-tinted views of how things are without the upstart start-ups. For this post's purpose the interesting question whether innovative business models will make ethical pressures stronger or weaker. I wouldn't like to speculate.

On one level, the 'we're better business people' schtick of the Innovators is a reason for thinking that things might get a bit worse. My own emphasis would not be on this broad, cultural indicator, indeed there is evidence from Parker et al ('The Two Faces of Lawyers: Professional Ethics and Business Compliance with Regulation') that lawyers can lead clients astray as often as vice versa. The important thing will be the kinds of business model that are run within innovative firms (which may directly incentivise particular kinds of behaviour) and the way in which staff are valued within such firms (of which the incentive structure is but one important part).

Innovative law firms have the opportunity to reconceptualise ownership, management and status within firms – so an interesting question is will they take that opportunity to design out the economic metricisation of individual performance and promotion.

Moving away from the idea that large proportions of your staff are in competition firstly for partnership and then for profit per partner has a lot to commend it. Can they do it and recruit the best staff, or good enough staff? Will they try? One glimmer of hope is Bill Henderson and Marc Galanter's research which suggests that what motivates young lawyers to stay with firms is not bonuses and salary levels but things like quality of work. Another is the research basis that suggests strong incentives diminish the motivation of those doing complex work. A re-negotiation of the human capital bargain may be possible but who's going to go first? BigLaw has too much to lose too quickly.

Let me push this question a little further. One of the ways that Innovators claim, with some justification, to be more ethical is through the challenge to the problems of exploitation and short termism associated with hourly billing. Yet there must be a worry that through swapping hourly billing for fixed fees one set of ethical problems is swapped for another. To deal with the economisation of practice argument first: law firms could just switch billable hours targets to fixed fees targets. The economic signal is still strong; the ethical risk remains heightened.

Proponents of fixed fees however like to emphasise how fixed fees shift some of the risk of legal work back on to providers. This better aligns lawyer and client interests and encourages more efficient or innovative responses to legal problems. What they really mean is they shift some of the risk of excessive cost back onto providers. What they tend not to mention is that fixed fees shift the risk of cutting corners back towards the client. But, c'est la vie and all that, the kinds of clients that are typically being talked about can assess that risk themselves. To which I would add: kind of, sort of. Again, there is utterly unsurprising evidence that fixed fees alter the lawyer's internal calculus of what work a job needs: do I need interview this witness is probably yes if it's an hourly fee, probably not if it's a fixed fee. This may not be all that sinister, the lawyer does not know whether interviewing the client will really be useful or not. And if the lawyer does not know, then I'm going to guess the client does not know either. The risk calculus is different, but no one knows whether it is better.

So in the short term innovation towards new pricing mechanisms poses risks to the client interests which may or may not be as serious as the risks posed by hourly fees. I reckon on the issues being somewhat less serious. My assumption being that fixed fees will help squeeze out some excess profit-taking on hourly bills which has nothing to do with protecting quality. Beyond that, mispricing and mismanagement of fixed fees will lead to corner-cutting on cases, and some more conventionally serious (but hopefully isolated) insolvency related ethical problems where whole business models crash because fixed fees have been mispriced.

The interesting thing for me about fixed fees though is the potential for them to reframe the way lawyers and clients think about law and legal services. Law firms will have to think about and predict cost much more finely. They and clients will have to weigh up the cost and benefits of building particular steps into any legal process. Both parties have strong interests in understanding value and achieving stable and predictable outcomes. The rather shallow notion of fixed fees being better for the client, and better aligning lawyer and client, will get deeper. Alignment may become more genuine. I am usually un-impressed by what I hear on value side of the equation; but occasionally I do sense more impressive and thoughtful approaches that harness systemisation and big data beyond the (not so simple) science of cost management and prediction. Now my sense is that value largely means getting from point A to B (in legal terms basically as we have always done) as quickly, efficiently and with as reassuring as sense of the quality of work as possible.

Better alignment will come when both sides have more than just a sense of value. Now, client and lawyer judgments about what really works are often (not always though) based on experience – a sometimes myopic, bias-ridden teacher but the best one available. Innovators genuinely looking to disrupt markets have to offer significant reassurance on the quality issue: they must work harder to show their products really work. That will drive a stronger, more evidence based interest in value and quality in the long run. Though again, innovators have every incentive (and are likely to be less opportunistically biased) to believe their own hype. They will overreach and fail; and sometimes succeed.

A final point is a return to the theme of values which we have touched on when thinking about money. Our own values influence ethical decision making. In broad terms our values can be reduced to two dimensions. Along one of these, we differ in how important extrinsic and intrinsic motivations (how interested in fairness and others we are vs how interested in our own status and rewards). Unsurprisingly, the latter is less likely to be ethical than the former. The Innovators will claim that they are better set up and incentivised to conceive of themselves as genuinely looking at the clients' needs. Whether the public interest in the administration of justice gets much of a look in, is more difficult to speculate on. The second dimension is the extent to which we are open to change or resists it in favour of security and tradition.

Broadly, as I understand it, the latter group is less likely to be associated with unethical behaviour. Innovators are more willing to try something different; and sometimes, like Canadian Mayors and Bankers on a night out that means they may be more willing to try things they shouldn't.

On the one hand, there seems little doubt that as a substitute, the NewLaw business model has a permanent and growing place in meeting many client needs. On the other hand, because the NewLaw journey is just beginning, it is premature to draw conclusions about the destiny of individual types of NewLaw firm.

In conclusion, it is apt to quote Peter Drucker: "The business enterprise has two – and only two – basic functions: marketing and innovation. Marketing and innovation produce results: All the rest are 'costs'." By 'marketing' Drucker means the identification and satisfaction of clients' needs. And by 'innovation' he means finding and executing strategies more cleverly than competitors. NewLaw, it seems to me, is following Drucker's guidance in both respects.

I trust our thread book – NewLaw New Rules – lives up to Peter Drucker's aphorism.

USEFUL SOURCES

Parker, Christine, Rosen, Robert, and Lehmann Nielsen, Vibecke, 'The Two Faces of Lawyers: Professional Ethics and Business Compliance with Regulation' (2009) 22 Georgetown Journal of Legal Ethics 201
http://papers.ssrn.com/sol3/papers.cfm?abstract_id=1034561

APPENDIX

CONTRIBUTORS

Joel Barolsky

It is clear the legal market, both in Australia and globally, is undergoing significant change. The claim that these changes will mean the end of

BigLaw firms and the wholesale replacement by NewLaw is both strategically naïve and is not backed up by any evidence.

Background
20+ years as strategy consultant and advisor to law and other professional services firms. Senior Fellow of The University of Melbourne and author of the Relationship Capital blog.

Current area of work/interest/specialisation

Developing agility and market sensing capabilities in a fast-changing competitive environment.

Exploring how firms can better identify, protect and leverage their relationship capital.

Loving the investment of time and energy in my son's cricket career.

http://www.relationshipcapital.com.au/

Nicole Bradick

There is concern over the future of training for lawyers if BigLaw continues to contract. NewLaw firms currently rely on BigLaw to train young lawyers and bless them with pedigree. The hope is that NewLaw of the future will train lawyers; when this occurs BigLaw may lose some of its attraction.

Background

Nicole Bradick was a litigator in a mid-sized firm until moving into the NewLaw arena after witnessing inefficiencies of traditional firm practice. Ms Bradick was honored as a "Legal Rebel" by the ABA Journal in 2012 after launching her first business, Custom Counsel.

Ms Bradick directs business development activities for Potomac Law Group, a NewLaw firm. She also runs Custom Counsel, a network of freelance lawyers that work with firms seeking help on a project basis.

I often conduct business with two toddlers attached to my legs.

http://www.potomaclawgrp.com/

Liam Brown

Liam founded Elevate in 2011.

Nimble, investor-backed NewLaw companies have filled the gap in the market left by slow-to-adapt BigLaw firms. But now they must deliver liquidity and ROI over the next few years as BigLaw leaders adopt NewLaw business model innovations, ranging from alternative resourcing to efficiency initiatives.

Background

Previously he was the Founder, President and CEO of Integreon, which he led from startup in 2001 to annual sales of $150 million by 2011.

Liam founded Elevate to provide corporate legal departments and law firms with practical ways to improve efficiency, quality and outcomes.

He is also an active investor in Web 2.0 and Cloud technologies for the legal sector, and an executive coach for founders of startups with Forward Accelerator.

http://www.elevateservices.com/

Eva Bruch

One of the brakes for innovation in the legal sector is in its own DNA: law firms are professional ones ruled by partnership systems such as the "eat what you kill" model that promote the individual economic interests of each partner to the detriment of the common good. The road to innovation includes managing this reality.

Background
Eva Bruch has a degree in Law and an MBA (EADA Business School, Barcelona). She worked as a lawyer and business developer for several firms in Spain.
She helps law firms finding a right strategy to achieve growth and innovation goals, advising as well in the use of technology to better manage the firm.

Triathlete and mother of two, Eva thinks everything is possible. Always with a pair of sneakers in her baggage when travelling.

http://www.morethanlaw.es/

Richard Burcher

'NewLaw' firms are characterised by amongst other things, high levels of sophistication around pricing governance. Analytics and execution not only yield higher profit margins and engender client loyalty and endorsement through a tangible demonstration of 'cost consciousness' and alignment of the firm's financial interests with those of clients.

Background

A former private practice lawyer of 30 years including seven years as managing partner, postgraduate study in pricing and a career long interest in the pricing of legal services.

Consulting to the international legal community on how to apply innovative and sophisticated pricing solutions to the delivery of legal services to maximise profitability and client satisfaction.

I still remember being told by the Dean of the Auckland law school in 1976 that based on my first semester exam marks, I might want to consider a career less intellectually demanding.

http://www.validatum.com/

Peter Carayiannis

We are witnessing a period of rapid evolution in the business and practice of law. There are evolutionary pressures coming from increasingly sophisticated clients who demand greater efficiency, more transparency, clearer accountability and something other than a 'time and materials' billable hour business model. With time we will see alternative and innovative legal services providers grow and flourish alongside traditional law firms. Those firms that recognise adaptation is the key to survival and everything revolves around providing the best value to the client will benefit.

Background

With a BA (Hons) from the University of Toronto (St Michael's College), a JD from Michigan State University and admitted to practice in both the US

(Michigan) and Canada (Ontario), Peter articled and practiced with Gowling Lafleur Henderson LLP. In 2004 he left Gowlings and began a practice as inhouse counsel on-demand. He founded Conduit Law Professional Corp, a Canadian law firm operating a distributed model, embedding corporate counsel as in-house lawyers in a variety of Canadian and multinational companies.

Rapidly building and expanding a national platform allowing high-tempo and highly experienced lawyers to work directly with sophisticated corporate clients.

Happily married, Peter is the father of three energetic young boys who spends his winter evenings maintaining a backyard ice rink.

http://www.conduitlaw.com/

Paul Carr

Awaiting the promise of widespread disruption.

Background

Paul was previously the General Manager of American Express' International Insurance Business, serviced as Amex's Global Head of Strategy, and a Partner at The Boston Consulting Group.

As President of Axiom, the world's largest and fastest growing provider of legal services, Paul Carr oversees the firm's global sales, service and delivery teams and is responsible for geographic expansion as well as service line development.

http://www.axiomlaw.com/

Greg Carter

The BigLaw business model relies on leverage for a large portion of its profit. The model is at risk to the extent NewLaw offers attractive alternative careers for lawyers.

Background

Barrister at the independent Bar, previously a commercial litigator at a national firm, prior to that an Aboriginal land rights/native title lawyer.

Building an online marketplace for legal services (LawyerSelect.com.au).

http://www.lawyerselect.com.au/

Karl Chapman

Innovative service providers can disrupt the legal market by leveraging the advantages that come from starting with a blank sheet. While an increase in in-house counsel saves in the short-term, professional outsourcers will be more efficient in the long run, as demonstrated by examples in recruitment.

Background

Chief Executive of Riverview Law. Founder and Chief Executive of AdviserPlus – a leading HR Advisory Outsourcing business. Set up CRT Group plc in 1989 which was a leading recruitment outsourcing business.

'Legal input. Business output.' Helping organisations change the way they use, measure and buy legal services.

Occasionally known to enjoy wine with friends!

http://www.riverviewlaw.com/

Eric Chin

Introduced the 'NewLaw' neologism as the antithesis of BigLaw. Speculated a future where Axiom, a NewLaw, may be the largest legal services firm by 2018. Studied the parasitical relationship between NewLaw and BigLaw and contrasted the business models.

Background

Analyst to the professions on strategy, structure, capital, acquisitions and disposals. His interest in the professions is showcased in the Beaton450 and Deal Monitor league tables, examining the world's largest accounting, engineering, law and management consulting firms, and tracking their acquisition patterns.

Works with senior management in the accounting, advisory and legal profession on corporate strategy and M&A assignments across Australia, New Zealand, Hong Kong, Singapore and other markets in the Asia-Pacific region.

http://www.beatoncapital.com/

Ross Dawson

Distributed legal services models have big potential to serve clients. Clients will choose between the efficiency offered by these newer models and the comfort and convenience offered by traditional law firms

Background

Ross worked in senior positions in London, Tokyo and Sydney with organisations including Merrill Lynch, NCR, and most recently Thomson Financial as Global Director-Capital Markets. He holds a Bachelor of Science (Hons) from Bristol University and a Graduate Diploma in Applied Finance from Macquarie University.

Ross is globally recognised as a leading futurist, keynote speaker, entrepreneur, and author on business strategy. He is Founding Chairman of four companies-international consulting and ventures firm Advanced Human Technologies, think tank Future Exploration Network, leading events firm The Insight Exchange, and online start-up Repyoot.

Ross speaks frequently at major conferences and company internal events around the world. He is a best-selling author of books including the prescient Living Networks, which foresaw the social networking revolution, as well as the blog Trends in the living Networks.

http://www.rossdawson.com/

James Edsberg

As the economic situation improves, the point of maximum pressure on the law firm business model has passed. Larger law firms can learn from the success of the 'Big 4'. These very large and diversified professional services firms provide a route map for large traditional law firms that want to keep pace with the needs of large and globalising clients.

Background

James Edsberg is a partner of Gulland Padfield, the strategy consultancy to the professional services sectors. The firm's teams have advised 30 of the leading 50 global law firms.

James authored clientcentricindix.com, an online diagnostic to help his law firm clients to benchmark and transform their profitability and performance through closer alignment to their clients and markets.

http://www.gullandpadfield.com/

Ron Friedmann

To achieve legal efficiency and improve value, changing the business model in NewLaw is not enough; lawyers must also change the way they practise law. All the opining about NewLaw trends is speculation; we lack almost any empirical data.

Background

Ron Friedmann is a consultant with Fireman & Company. He improves law practice efficiency and law firm business operations. He is a lawyer and former BigLaw CIO.

Knowledge management, legal project management, legal and business process outsourcing, e-discovery, process improvement, online legal services, legal vendor marketing, and technology for law practice and law firm operations.

All my addictions turn out to be healthy: reading general and legal news, exercise, and dark chocolate.

http://www.prismlegal.com/

Jordan Furlong

Large law firms are facing a near-complete transformation of their business models and are mostly ill-equipped to see this process through. Large firm associate training is designed to produce law firm employees, not entrepreneurial lawyers of the future.

Background

Lawyer, author, speaker, consultant, and legal industry analyst analyzing the trends underway in the global legal market and advising market participants on adaptation strategies.

Lawyer, author, speaker, consultant, and legal industry analyst analyzing the trends underway in the global legal market and advising market participants on adaptation strategies.

Former legal journalist, sci-fi devotee, gaming addict, Whovian, father of two, husband of one, last remaining fan of Supertramp.

http://www.law21.ca/

Kenneth A. Grady

Changes affecting the legal services industry are not unique; most industries have experienced similar disruptions. Rather than obsessing about these changes, BigLaw should use them as the opportunity to re-invent themselves. Now is the time for BigLaw to win back the role of C-suite trusted advisor.

Background

Ken's experience includes partnership in a major, multinational law firm and 20-years in-house experience including general counsel and executive roles with Fortune 1000 corporations.

Ken is CEO of SeyfarthLean Consulting LLC. He helps law departments achieve strategic and operational excellence, and develops tailored solutions improving the efficiency and effectiveness of law department performance.

Ken is an avid orchardist and ruralist spending his free time rejuvenating an heirloom apple orchard.

http://www.seyfarth.com /

Andrew Grech

Across the legal services landscape the convergence of evolving client demand (at individual, SME, corporate and government levels), changing client socio-demographics across regions and the emergence of technology which enables services to be delivered with improved value are starting to have a profound impact on the legal profession. The process of change is accelerating and bringing many opportunities to meet clients' needs innovatively, professionally and affordably.

Background
Group Managing Director of Slater & Gordon Ltd.

As Group Managing Director of Slater & Gordon Ltd I focus my time on the achievement of our goal – to provide world class legal services to everyday people.

http://www.slatergordon.com.au/

John Grimley

BigLaw has the ability to create demand for its own services.

Management consultant to law firms on cross-border business development strategy. US lawyer, former Director, AM Law 100 Law Firm, Patton to GGS LLP European Business Development office.

Cross-border business development strategic advisor to law firms, law firm practice group and individual practitioners.

http://internationalbusinessdevelopmentblog.com/

Susan Hackett

While it is critical to focus our attention on the changing NewLaw firm business model, it is equally critical to remain grounded in developing solutions that are aligned with client needs and perspectives. In this exchange, Susan reminds us that law firms who confuse clients who have always sent them business with clients who are satisfied with the work are making a dangerous assumption.

Background

Having served for more than two decades as the General Counsel of the Association of Corporate Counsel, Susan Hackett is one of the world's leading experts on in-house practice in its many forms: across industries, geographies, and subject matter.

Susan Hackett is the CEO of a consulting firm specializing in law department and law firm leadership and management: Legal Executive Leadership, LLC.

Corporate clients don't have legal problems, they have business problems. To serve them well, you must be more than a good lawyer; you must be a good business executive.

http://www.legalexecutiveleadership.com/2011/susan hackett/

Silvia Hodges Silverstein

The key questions for the New Legal curriculum are:

1) How do we educate future generations of lawyers so they are prepared to succeed in 2020 and beyond? and
2) What will the role of the lawyer be in 2020?

Thinking like a lawyer needs to be thinking like a value-creating legal issues problem-solver.

Background

Dr Silvia Hodges Silverstein connects her decade of field-based research with first-hand experiences working in-house in law firms and advising legal departments to generate novel insights and practical recommendations.

She researches, teaches, speaks and advises on purchasing decisions, legal procurement, metrics, marketing/business development, and change in law firms. Silvia co-authored a HBS case on GlaxoSmithKline's sourcing of legal services.

http://www.silviahodges.com/

Trish Hyde

In-house counsel have more options than ever before to exercise their buying power.

Trish Hyde is CEO of the Australian Corporate Lawyers Association.

She has over 15 years senior corporate management experience across a broad range of industries.

Trish holds a Master Commercial Law & Master Corporate Leadership.

http://www.acla.com.au/

Ken Jagger

There is a need for traditional law firms to restructure their business models to meet client demands.

Ken is CEO of AdventBalance.

He was a partner of Freehills, now Herbert Smith Freehills.

http://www.adventbalance.com/

Imme Kaschner

Secular trends in the legal services industry necessitate changes in legal education both prior to and after graduation. A recent New York City Bar report 'Developing legal careers and developing justice in the 21st century' shows there are feasible options to do this. Early in-house training, and setting up new structures to address unmet civil legal needs with appropriate supervision, open new ways of early-career legal training.

Background

Recent JD (The University of Melbourne) graduate, medical doctor and researcher, intellectual property law aficionado.

Imme is a Research Assistant with Beaton Capital.

Learning to kite-board, occasionally successfully combining both kiting and boarding.

Imme Kaschner on LinkedIn

Mitch Kowalski

The changes happening within the legal services industry are structural, not cyclical.

Mitch Kowalski is a lawyer, consultant and the author of the critically acclaimed American Bar Association best seller, "Avoiding Extinction: Reimagining Legal Services for the 21st Century".

http://www.kowalski.ca/

Joshua Kubicki

No lawyer or law firm can change business model without new technologies and processes. Those who want change need to invest in creating, supporting and using new tools. The start-up part of the legal ecosystem is growing because of this.

Background

Joshua founded the Legal Transformation Institute, a business design firm, and Law Angels, an investment network focused on early-stage legal startups. Both focus on building, launching, and fueling new businesses and business models within the legal market.

Executing and enabling growth for Early-stage to Private Equity/Ventured backed companies within the global legal economy.

I am not about the "end of lawyers," I am about empowering lawyers to more fully participate in the expanding and diversifying global legal industry.

http://www.transformlegal.com/

Patrick Lamb

Law firms and in-house law departments are also subject to the business pressures client organisations encounter daily. There will be some winners and many losers among firms in the competition for talent and clients.

These forces are generating massive pressure for change, with the outcome being a very different world, now known as the New Normal.

Background

I am a BigLaw refugee who founded Valorem with three friends. We service the corporate world doing complex litigation on a non-hourly basis.

Alternative Business Systems and the role of capital in helping New Normal firms reach their potential to provide greater value to clients.

Just completed a book draft for American Bar Association on alternative fees. Coming next quarter.

http://www.valoremlaw.com/

Dan Lear

Young lawyers are interested in new 'virtual' workplaces, but training opportunities are scarce.

Background

I'm a fifth year attorney in Seattle. I've spent most of my legal career at a version of "NewLaw" firms. I'm passionate about the changing legal industry. Co-founder of Seattle Legal Innovation and Technology MeetUp. Blogger at http://right-brain-law.blogspot.com/

Current area of work/interest/specialisation Tech lawyer.

Aspirational job: Changing the legal industry to make it more accessible, meaningful, and effective for legal professionals, clients, and the general public.

Father of three boys. Never been to Australia or met George in person but couldn't be more pleased to be virtually acquainted with him.

http://right-brain-law.blogspot.com/

Derek Minus

Australian lawyers see changes as an 'overseas thing'.

Background

Barrister with a specialist practice in the resolution of disputes by

Appropriate Dispute Resolution methods. Also a Nationally Accredited Mediator and a Chartered Arbitrator with significant expertise in these areas.

Current area of work/interest/specialisation

Practising in commercial mediation and arbitration.

http://www.medarb.com/

Richard Moorhead

In examining the BigLaw-NewLaw contrast in ethical terms we should view neither business model through rose-tinted spectacles and be mindful the impact of economic incentives on ethical standards of behaviour.

Background

Richard is Director of the UCL Centre for Ethics and Law in the Faculty of

Laws. He is an academic and former solicitor who has spent his career researching lawyers, legal services and access to justice.

Current area of work/interest/specialisation

Regulation of legal services; innovation; professional ethics and access to justice.

His blog, lawyerwatch, has been described as a must read for policy makers in legal services as well as the Thunderer.

http://www.lawyerwatch.wordpress.com/

Warren Riddell

'The future isn't what it used to be'. Client power is reshaping the BigLaw business model. BigLaw is in future shock and change is inevitable.

Background
Over 25 years of experience, has had leadership roles in the professions and in industry in Europe, Middle East, Asia-Pacific and North America, with a focus on new market development.

Current area of work/interest/specialisation
Partner in Beaton Capital and Director of Beaton Research + Consulting, specialist in new market strategy, development and acquisition with an interest innovation. More recently he has led a number of M&A mandates.

Always keen to learn more, currently working on my second masters and I will be a guest lecturer at Sydney University Business School in 2014.

http://www.beatoncapital.com/

Nick Seddon

BigLaw and NewLaw are separated by many shades of grey. The reaction of the firms that make up BigLaw to the ever-changing environment is what will determine whether they survive and whether they thrive or get swallowed up, but within the next 20 years, I see fast evolution rather than revolution.

Background

Until recently, headed the Asia region for Eversheds, based in Hong Kong. Prior to moving into a predominantly management role he was a corporate lawyer who handled a variety of transactions.

Recently joined Beaton Capital as a partner.

http://www.beatoncapital.com/

Richard Susskind

If one leading law firm breaks rank and delivers world-class service at significantly lower cost, using alternative methods of sourcing, then the market will change irreversibly.

Background

Professor Richard Susskind OBE is an author, speaker and independent adviser to major professional firms and to national governments. His main area of expertise is the future of professional service and, in particular, the way in which the IT and the Internet are changing the work of lawyers.

Recently published 'Tomorrow's Lawyers – An Introduction to Your Future' (OUP 2013).

http://www.susskind.com/

Jeremy Szwider

NewLaw is about a revolution in the legal market place. Alternative business models (such as LPOs, online legal marketplaces, virtual law firms, commoditisation, etc.) are evidence of this. In some NewLaw firms, the

distinction between private practice and in-house is increasingly blurred – incorporating the best aspects of both worlds.

Background
Jeremy has worked in both private practice at Australian and UK law firms (such as LDA Piper) and as a General Counsel of a FTSE 100 company in the UK (Car phone Warehouse and AOL group of companies). Jeremy is the Founder and Managing

Director Bespoke Law, an exciting platform to showcase a new model of law firm.

Current area of work/interest/specialisation
Lawyer & Outsourced In-House Counsel for growth businesses. Founder and Managing Director at Bespoke Law.

www.bespokelaw.com/

Steven Tyndall

BigLaw typically asks 'How can I use technology to do what I do better?' Whereas NewLaw simply asks 'How can it be done better?'.

Background

15 years of ICT experience, seven 7 in Legal IT. Current role: Group Manager – Technology and Information Systems @McCullough Robertson, previously IT Manager @Lander & Rogers.

Current area of work/interest/specialisation Legal technology, innovation and strategy.

Steven Tyndall on LinkedIn

Noah Waisberg

My response to a comment to the post was centred on whether "well-run incumbent law firms [would] blindly [watch] their profits halve ... without adjusting their cost base and adapting their ways." While this may seem unlikely, The Innovator's Dilemma describes this happening.

Background

CEO of DiligenceEngine, a company with software that helps lawyers review contracts faster and more accurately. Previously, Noah was a corporate lawyer in Weil, Gotshal's New York office.

Current area of work/interest/specialisation
Corporate lawyer enhancement; legal automation.

http://blog.diligenceengine.com/

EXAMPLES OF NEWLAW FIRMS

Firm	Top management	Country	Tagline
AdventBalance Founded 2008	Ken Jagger John Knox	AUSTRALIA Head office: Perth	*Bringing new life to law*
	www.adventbalance.com		
Axiom Law Founded 2000	Mark Harris Alec Guettel	USA Head office: Washington	*Law redefined*
	www.axiomlaw.com *Twitter handle:* @Axiom_Law		
Bespoke Law Founded 2009	Jeremy Szwider	AUSTRALIA Head office: Melbourne	*Your future law firm*
	www.bespokelaw.com/Home *Twitter handle:* @BespokeLaw		
Clearspire Founded 2008	Mark Cohen Bryce Arrowood	USA Head office: Washington	*Law practice. Reengineered*
	www.clearspire.com *Twitter handle:* @clearspire		
Cognition LLP Founded 2005	Joe Milstone Rubsun Ho	CANADA Head office: Toronto	*At Cognition, we do business differently.*
	www.cognitionllp.com *Twitter handle:* @CognitionLLP		
Conduit Law Founded 2012	Peter Carayiannis	CANADA Head office: Toronto	*The evolution of law*
	www.conduitlaw.com *Twitter handle:* @Conduit_Law		

Firm	Top management	Country	Tagline
CPA Global Founded 1969	Peter Sewell	UK Head office: Jersey	*Intellectual property solutions and Legal support services*
	www.cpaglobal.com *Twitter handle:* @CPAGlobal		
Epoq Founded 1994	Grahame Cohen Richard Cohen Hillel Horwitz	UK Head office: London	*Making law easy*
	www.epoq.co.uk *Twitter handle:* @epoq		
Exigent LPO Founded 2003	David Holme	SOUTH AFRICA Head office: Cape Town	*An intelligent alternative*
	www.exigentlpo.com *Twitter handle:* @ExigentGlobal		
GreenPoint Legal Founded 2005	Sanjay Sharma Jacklyn Karceski	USA Head office: New York	*Global legal services firm simplifying, supporting and enabling the business of law for our clients in 50+ countries and 50+ languages.*
	www.gplegalservices.com *Twitter handle:* @GreenPointLegal		
Inovia Founded 2002	Justin Simpson David Nelson	USA Head office: New York	*The global leader in foreign patent filing*
	www.inovia.com *Twitter handle:* @inoviaIP		
LawDepot Founded 2002	Ken Sawyer	CANADA Head office: Edmonton	*Easy legal forms in minutes*
	www.lawdepot.com *Twitter handle:* @LawDepot		

Firm	Top management	Country	Tagline
LawPath Founded 2013	Paul Lupson Andy Rose Damien Andreasen	AUSTRALIA Head office: Sydney	*Legal made easy*
	www.lawpath.com.au/smbs *Twitter handle:* @LawPath		
LawTrades Founded 2013	Raad Ahmed	USA Head office: New York	*Legal tech startup*
	www.lawtrades.com *Twitter handle:* @LawTrades		
LawyerSelect Founded 2013	Greg Carter	AUSTRALIA Head office: Perth	*Australia's online marketplace for legal talent*
	www.lawyerselect.com.au *Twitter handle:* @LawyerSelect		
LegalMatch Founded 1999	Laurie Ziffrin Anna Ostrovsk	USA Head office: San Francisco	*Find the right lawyer now*
	www.legalmatch.com *Twitter handle:* @LegalMatch		
LegalZoom Founded 2001	Eddie Hartman Brian Liu Robert Shapiro Brian Lee	USA Head office: Los Angeles	*Affordable. Personalized. Protection.*
	www.legalzoom.com *Twitter handle:* @LegalZoom		
Novus Law Founded 2005	Raymond Bayley	USA Head office: Chicago	*The measure of certainty*
	www.novuslaw.com *Twitter handle:* @NovusLawLLC		
Pangea3 Founded 2004	Sanjay Kamlani David Perla	USA/INDIA Head office: New York/Mumbai	*The global leader in legal outsourcing*
	www.pangea3.com *Twitter handle:* @Pangea3		

Firm	Top management	Country	Tagline
Plexus Legal Founded 2010	Andrew Mellett	AUSTRALIA Head office: Melbourne	*Transforming the value of legal services*
	www.plxs.com.au		
Riverview Law Founded 2011	Karl Chapman Adam Shutkever	UK Head office: Liverpool	*Legal advice for a fixed fee*
	www.riverviewlaw.com *Twitter handle:* @RiverviewLaw		
Rocket Lawyer Founded 2008	Charley Moore Dan Nye	USA Head office: San Francisco	*Everything you need to make it legal.*
	www.rocketlawyer.com *Twitter handle:* @RocketLawyer		
Shake Law Founded 2012	Abe Geiger	USA Head office: New York	*Simply legal*
	www.shakelaw.com *Twitter handle:* @ShakeLaw		
Slater & Gordon Founded 2007	Andrew Grech	AUSTRALIA Head office: Melbourne	*Not a problem*
	www.slatergordon.com.au *Twitter handle:* @SlaterGordon		
Trademarkia Founded 2009	Raj Abhyanker Dongxia Liu	USA Head office: San Francisco	*The largest search engine for trademarks*
	www.trademarkia.com *Twitter handle:* @Trademarkia		

THE AUTHOR

George Beaton

NewLaw New Rules breaks new ground. Our book shows how trends in industry structure and clients' buying behaviour are changing the legal landscape – and in doing so creating opportunities for a new category of legal services provider and challenging law firms based on the traditional business model.

Background

Legal services industry specialist | Business adviser to law firms Leader of strategy and research consultancies serving professional services firms.

Author | Commentator | Keynote speaker

In the recent past a senior member of the Melbourne Business School and the Melbourne Law School in The University of Melbourne.

In the distant past a medical school professor in the University of the Witwatersrand, South Africa

Current area of work/interest/specialisation

Globalisation of professional services

Contemporary meaning of professionalism

Fulfilled husband, father and grandfather

http://www.beatoncapital.com/
http://www.beatonglobal.com/
http://www.law.unimelb.edu.au/

www.ingramcontent.com/pod-product-compliance
Lightning Source LLC
Chambersburg PA
CBHW030934220326
41521CB00040B/2306